MW00648740

"I meet thousands of pastors and ⌐ his family really stand out. One of those 'Wise beyond his years' kind of guys. His heart to walk with Jesus and love others alongside Jesus is contagious. Jeff texts a group of people every Monday morning asking how he can pray for them that week. All to say, I'm thankful for Jeff and trust that you'll be greatly encouraged by this book!"

TIM TIMMONS
Contemporary Christian Music Songwriter & Recording Artist

"While saying that worship is more than music might sound trite, I don't know that anyone would argue that Jesus wasn't a worship leader, and yet we only find one account in all four Gospels of Jesus actually singing. Jesus made it clear. He came to glorify the Father, and He invited His followers to glorify the Father together with Him. While Jeff is an incredibly gifted musician, worship leading for him is about so much more than just making great music. This book is a reflection of that. For Jeff, worship leading is a way of inviting others into the journey of becoming passionate followers of Jesus and discipling the team that helps you do that. Worship that doesn't lead to or flow out of a life of obedience isn't a reflection of the disciple-making, Father-glorifying heart of Jesus. Jeff is uniquely gifted to equip fellow worship leaders in discipling their worship teams and leading worshipers to become fully devoted followers of Jesus."

DOUG HOLLIDAY
Executive Director, Sonlife Ministries

"Jeff Polen is a worship leader as well as a mentor to worship teams. He knows how to lead a worship team that will, in turn, lead a congregation (or a stadium) to the throne of God so that when the Word is proclaimed, the ground (ahem... the heart) is softened and receptive to the seed (the Word of God). The thoughts and principles in this book will help a worship 'band' become a worship 'team.' "

JOHN SCHMID
Recording Artist, Author, Founder of Common Ground Ministries

"I am not a worship leader (or the son of a worship leader), but this book articulates much of what I've felt in my heart for years when it comes to worship and worship leading. As a former pastor and current evangelist, I've been around all sorts of worship teams and leaders. The best ones disappear. They have me so focused on Christ that I forget they are even there... and so does the audience. This book will help you become invisible to those you are leading in worship and will put the spotlight on King Jesus. It's full of points that are practical and powerful. I highly recommend this book to all worship teams and worship leaders!"

GREG STIER
Founder, CEO Dare 2 Share

"Jeff Polen, where have you been all my life? If I had read this when I was a kid, maybe I could've been a musician! Seriously, Jeff has done every church and every worship leader, along with every musician and vocalist, a great favor. *#WeeklyWorshipThoughts* is a MUST READ! It is informative, educational, and motivational. If you are a pastor, buy a copy for every member in the worship team. If you are the worship leader, get a copy for your whole team, including the person running sound. If you're on the team, go get a copy for yourself. I could not be more serious. I believe this book has the potential of taking you and your team to another level, which will, in turn, take the entire worship experience of your church to a whole new level."

STEVE WINGFIELD
Evangelist, Author

"Jeff is not just a worship leader, he is a lead worshiper. His passion to bring others along in his worship of God is clearly seen and felt in the way he leads. He is a guy who is sensitive to the Spirit's leading, and I personally have been blessed by his ministry."

ZANE BLACK
Author & Speaker | Founder of Lov'n Life Ministries

#WEEKLY WORSHIP THOUGHTS

ENHANCING YOUR COLLECTIVE WORSHIP

JEFF POLEN

Illustrations by: Brooke Gehman

JPV PRESS

Copyright © 2019 JPV Press

All rights reserved. No part of this publication may be reproduced, distributed, or transmitted in any form or by any means, including photocopying, recording, or other electronic or mechanical methods, without the prior written permission of the publisher, except in the case of brief quotations embodied in critical reviews and certain other noncommercial uses permitted by copyright law.

Scripture quotations are from The ESV® Bible (The Holy Bible, English Standard Version®), copyright © 2001 by Crossway, a publishing ministry of Good News Publishers. Used by permission. All rights reserved. All Scriptures that are not in ESV are noted with correct version.

Illustrations by Brooke Gehman.

Printed in the United States of America

First Printing, 2019

ISBN 978-1-946389-16-9

JPV PRESS

STORY. PRESERVED.

2106 Main Street / PO Box 201, Winesburg, OH 44690

www.jpvpress.com

DEDICATION

TO EVERY WORSHIP TEAM MEMBER, WORSHIP LEADER, PASTOR, MINISTRY LEADER, AND LAYPERSON WITH WHICH I HAVE HAD, AND WILL HAVE, THE PLEASURE (AND THE PAIN) OF WORKING... THIS BOOK REALLY IS FOR YOU, AND FROM YOU. I HOPE IT HELPS!

HE GAVE THE APOSTLES, THE PROPHETS, THE EVANGELISTS, THE SHEPHERDS AND TEACHERS, TO EQUIP THE SAINTS FOR THE WORK OF MINISTRY, FOR BUILDING UP THE BODY OF CHRIST, UNTIL WE ALL ATTAIN TO THE UNITY OF THE FAITH AND OF THE KNOWLEDGE OF THE SON OF GOD, TO MATURE MANHOOD, TO THE MEASURE OF THE STATURE OF THE FULLNESS OF CHRIST. (EPHESIANS 4:11-13)

CONTENTS

PREFACE

Wow! It is hard to believe that I have been leading worship for nearly two decades! I served as "Music Director" (though I much preferred the term "Worship Pastor") at a church in Ohio for ten years. Prior to that, I had spent more than a decade of my life playing secular music and touring the country, playing over 100 shows per year. It has been a wild ride, and God is not finished with me yet!

The past few years have probably been the most exciting for me, personally. In January of 2017, my wife and I became full-time "Musicianaries" (Musical Missionaries) with the Jeff Polen Music Ministry.

As much as I enjoy life as a Musicianary (and I certainly feel called by God to it), there is an undeniable hole in my heart. Something is missing. That "something" is the ability to speak into the lives of worshipers on a weekly basis.

As a music director, I looked forward to Thursday evenings, when we would get together as a worship team to rehearse for the upcoming Sunday morning service. That was a high calling, for sure. I never saw my responsibility as merely making preparations for Sunday morning, but rather, as an opportunity to grow as a worshiper and to invest in those worshiping around me.

My "#ThursdayWorshipThoughts," which originally appeared on my blog at www.jeffpolenmusic.com every Thursday morning throughout 2018, were a way for me to continue along this journey of investing in worshipers. I might not have been leading worship at the same church every Sunday as I once did, but this outlet gave me the opportunity to form a "cyber church" of sorts.

Throughout the year, I drew upon my own experiences, successes, and failures as I posted my #ThursdayWorshipThoughts. Part of my calling as a Musicianary, after all, is to offer training and resources.

Brooke Gehman, one of my favorite guys in the whole world, joined me for the epic endeavor of bringing this book to life by offering a fun, artistic representation of the central point for each chapter. Brooke and I met at Youth With A Mission (YWAM) Nashville in 2005. He is an authentic and wonderful man of God, a devoted follower of Christ, and an amazing husband and father. He is a gifted worship leader, a potter by trade (check out his website: www.gehmanpottery.com), and an incredible artist.

The #ThursdayWorshipThoughts blog posts, which became the individual chapters of this book, were not necessarily meant to talk about what we were doing right. They were more often written to highlight areas of improvement. I considered this to be the most helpful approach.

In 2015, I took a three-month Sabbatical from the church where I was serving. I used this time away from normal church duties as an opportunity to take professional recording classes. I spent seven 80-hour weeks learning how to record music professionally. I did not consider myself to be a novice at this point, but I was by no means a pro, either.

During my classes, I discovered three basic categories of things that I was learning.

1.) There were things that I already knew. This category was fun because it was encouraging to know that I was actually doing something right!

2.) There were things that I didn't know. This category hurt a little bit. If there was to be any hope of change—and, ultimately, of doing things right—I had to admit that I was doing things wrong.

3.) Then, there were the things that I didn't know I didn't know. This was the most unexpected category! Though I had been in and around recording studios for more than half my life, there were so many things that I didn't know I didn't know. In fact, I'm not even sure what questions I could have asked in order to accumulate the right information.

My hope for the weekly #ThursdayWorshipThoughts blog was for each idea to fit into one of those three basic categories. I was hoping the readers, as worship leaders or worship team members, would read the blog and realize they were doing something right. Great! Or perhaps they would read and be convicted of areas where they were not quite doing it right—in fact, maybe they were doing it wrong. That can be helpful, too. And, I think it is highly likely that many readers encountered something in the weekly blog that illuminated ideas they didn't know they didn't know. Fantastic!

The book you are holding in your hands is simply the collection of my weekly #ThursdayWorshipThoughts compiled throughout 2018. I believe they provided helpful insights to my blog followers in 2018, but I also believe they are timeless truths that can have a positive impact on worship teams across the country.

My hope for this book is that worship teams will work through it together, chapter by chapter. I recommend that each member of the team have their own copy of the book, read the chapter on their own, and then come together as a team to process what they are learning. I believe these chapters will help provide the basis for amazing group discussions. That would be a huge win!

Perhaps some of the chapters will not directly apply to you. That's okay; it won't hurt to think through that subject together anyway. Perhaps some of the ideas will generate strong disagreement. That's okay, too! At least you can come to the point as a team where you know what you believe, and why. Perhaps some of the ideas are things that the worship leader or individual worship team members have has been wanting to say but didn't know how to bring it up. I am happy to be the one who is able to do so; feel free to use me as the scapegoat.

While my primary hope is that entire worship teams will use this book as they process, learn, and grow together, I do not consider the book to be exclusively for worship teams. As with the weekly blog, perhaps senior pastors, laypersons, or even non-Christians will find it to be helpful in some way, shape, or form. Great! My God is able to accomplish infinitely more than I might ask or think! (see Ephesians 3:20)

As a full-time Musicianary, one of the things I love to do is come alongside church worship teams and worship leaders to assist (dare I say "disciple") them into becoming the worship team that God created them to be. I think this book can go a long way toward making that a reality, but I also envision a significant number of questions popping up for worship teams and worship leaders who begin to put what I say into practical use. I would love to help further unpack some of these best practices, or truths.

I will know the book is really clicking when I am asked to speak to worship teams or congregations, and they say, "Can you talk a little more about chapter X, and Y, and XY?"

Yes, I can. And I would love to.

- JEFF POLEN

MUSICIANS, GOD IS OMNIPRESENT—YOU ARE NOT

Where shall I go from your Spirit? Or where shall I flee from your presence? If I ascend to heaven, you are there! If I make my bed in Sheol, you are there! (Psalm 139:7-8)

God is omnipresent. That means He is present everywhere, all of the time. This is a great and awesome truth about God, but it is one of His attributes that we are not meant to emulate!

I was once asked to play electric guitar for a worship leader that I know, and I was happy to do so. It was a fairly small band (acoustic guitar, bass guitar, electric guitar, keyboard, and vocals), and this particular worship leader is also a recording artist whose music is primarily acoustic and electric guitar-driven. It sounded like fun, and I was glad to help.

I spent several days prior to the event listening through the recordings of the songs from the set list, learning the electric guitar parts. My desire, as a musician, was to serve both the worship leader and the songs by playing my parts well. By the day of the event, I was ready!

It wasn't until sound check that I realized there was a problem. The acoustic guitar player was playing their part. The bass guitar player was playing their part. As the electric guitar player, I was playing my part. The keyboard player... well, the keyboard player was actually playing ALL of our parts.

I could not find a helpful way to contribute to the songs. I listened to the keyboard, and sure enough, with the power of their right and left hand combined, they had the bass, low-mids, high-mids, and highs completely covered. The keyboard was omnipresent!

The bass guitar was in a great groove, but it didn't matter. Their notes were covered up and constantly competing with the keys. The acoustic guitar player was laying down a strong rhythm, but it didn't matter; their chords were covered up. I tried to play in every register available to the electric guitar but soon realized that it didn't matter if I played high, low, or in between; the keyboard was already there!

Where shall I flee from your presence?

I attempted to just play the musical runs at the end of each phrase (the ones that I learned by listening to the recordings), but the keyboard player was actively inventing their own runs for the end of each phrase. In one final attempt to make a positive contribution, I tried to just swell nice chords into the songs, but the keyboard player was using a musical pad that sonically swallowed up literally everything I tried.

The keyboard was present everywhere, all the time.

As for skill, there is no question that the keyboard player knew how to play their instrument. What they did not know was how to play their part and actually fit in with other musicians.

One of the principles that I teach regarding worship is the idea that the best musicians have the biggest ears. I don't mean the physical size of the musician's ear, of course, but I do mean the physical use of their ear. Good musicians listen critically to what the other musicians are contributing to the song so that they know how to fit in and enhance what is happening musically. God is the only One who is meant to be omnipresent.

After sound check, I spoke with the sound man, who informed me that he had pulled the keyboard almost completely out of the mix.

"Why?" I asked.

"He was everywhere, man!"

NOTES

WORSHIP LEADERS,
HELP THE PEOPLE SING!

When you tune in to songs on the radio, what do you hear? If you listen to the same radio station for any length of time, you will notice that you hear basically the same songs over and over. This is good! It happens that way on purpose.

The radio stations have figured out that people generally want to hear the same songs over and over. Occasionally there is a new song, but for the most part, people want to hear a song often enough to memorize the words and sing along. Not only that, but people actually want to have the song playing in their head throughout the day. They want to talk with their friends and family about the song they love and have them tune in to the same station to hear it for themselves.

Again, this is good!

Now, when you come to worship the Lord through music in church, what do you hear? If you go to the same church for several weeks, months, and years in a row, too often you will hear far too many songs. This is bad.

Too many worship leaders wonder why their congregations are not passionately singing along. The answer is simple; the congregation hasn't heard the songs often enough. They hear a completely different set of songs each week, many of which are really not that great. If the lyrics were not projected onto the screen, the congregation would have no idea of how to join in. About the time they finally learn how to sing the song (because it was played once or twice a quarter for a couple of years), the song is now considered too old to be effective.

Again, this is bad!

Sure, some people like Pandora, but that's mostly just musical people. The church is not filled with musical people. The church is filled with people from all walks of life. Some are musical, but most are not. Still, ALL of God's people are called to worship Him through music. (There is actually a whole book of the Bible devoted to it.) As worship leaders, we need to help them sing!

If radio stations operated like churches with their song playlist, they would go out of business. People would stop advertising on the radio because no one would tune in.

Unfortunately, many of the worshipers who come to church on Sunday morning are no longer "tuning in," as well. Many of them want to, but we have made it too difficult for them. Even many of our musically talented worship team members have a hard time tuning in because each week they have to learn a completely different set of songs.

There is a better way.

Worship leaders, take your cue from the success of radio and help people sing. Prune that song list down to no more than forty songs per season. Choose great songs and only great songs! Make sure those great songs show up for multiple seasons, give them a season-long break, and then bring them back.

Your job isn't to spin our heads and leave us breathless by the amazing amount of songs that you can play (while staring at a song sheet). Your job is to lead us into an awareness of the presence and glory of God by leading us in songs that we know, love, have sung a hundred times, and can declare passionately this week as we anticipate singing it again soon... just as if the song were on the radio.

NOTES

THERE IS A
BLESSING IN THE BOREDOM

One of the most common critiques of church worship music that I hear from worship team members (especially those members whose personal playlist does NOT include church worship songs) is that the songs are "too easy." They claim that the songs are boring.

Hmm...

One of my own most common critiques of many worship team members is that they are "too busy" on their instrument. They feel that the songs need spicing up, so the drummer adds triplet fills at the end of every measure, the bass player adds runs to every root note, the acoustic guitarist becomes the main rhythm section, and the electric guitarist and keyboard player play every possible note within the given scale (and several notes that are very much not a part of the scale). Why do they do this? They claim that the songs are boring.

Hmm...

First off, if songs about the omnipotent, omnipresent, omniscient, eternal God and Creator of everything that we see, feel, touch, hear, smell, taste, and imagine (and more!) are boring to you, then I would suggest that you are missing the point.

Second, if somehow you recognize the vast greatness of the One of whom you are singing and are still bored, I would submit that there is a blessing in the boredom.

As worship leaders or worship team members, our priority is not personal stimulation. Our priority is serving. As worship team members, we have the awesome privilege of serving the song, serving the worship leader, serving the congregation, and serving God! We are not standing on the stage to fulfill our own desire to be entertained. We have been given the awesome privilege of leading God's people into an awareness of the presence and glory of God. (How is that boring?)

Nevertheless, if the songs are easy to play, good! (Unless we are talking about Classical compositions or Jazz, most genres are not too difficult to play once you are used to them.) The fact that the songs are easy to play is actually a blessing. That just means you can spend more energy on the things that really matter. There truly is a blessing in the boredom!

Go ahead and play the song the way it was meant to be played, without all the extra nonsense. Since you don't have to think so hard about the extra—and often unhelpful—notes, why not spend your extra mental energy meditating on the words of the song? Why not sing along, and make the song your own prayer to God? Surely you can do that while playing such easy songs.

Why not memorize the songs and get rid of that unnecessary music stand altogether? Without that beginners-level barrier in the way—the one to which your eyes are so frequently glued—you can now focus on intentionally connecting with the congregation. (Remember them?) Make eye contact with them. Smile. Let them know you are happy to see them.

While you're at it, why not pick out specific people, names, and faces in the congregation and pray over them as you simply provide songs to which they can also sing and pray along? Your extra notes, fills, and rhythmic intricacies are actually not improving their situation in any way whatsoever.

So go ahead and embrace the blessing in the boredom. Thank God that singing songs about His infinite goodness is not an overly difficult task. Amid the boredom, focus on what really matters.

NOTES

4

PLAN FOR
THE WEAKEST LINK

I used to work construction for a living. Chains were a tool we would use on a daily basis. We used chains to lift, pull, or hold items as we worked, and I found out quickly that a chain is only as strong as its weakest link. You could only lift, pull or hold items that the weakest link could handle. If that link of the chain was pushed beyond its ability, everything came crumbling down.

I think it is helpful to consider this basic concept when leading a worship team: plan for the weakest link.

This concept may sound derogatory, but it is not meant to be. It is meant to be exceptionally helpful and loving.

The reality is that many of us worship leaders are working with volunteer musicians. Perhaps you are in a situation where you are working

13

with paid, professional musicians, but most of us are not. Church leadership may task us with the responsibility of providing musical worship for the congregation, but that is not our primary calling. Our primary calling comes straight from the Lord Jesus, and it is to make disciples! When you realize this, it becomes imperative that you plan for the weakest link.

Practically speaking, I mean to say that the songs we select and the arrangements we put together should be considerate of the actual musicians on our worship team—especially the member with the lowest skill level.

We may be blessed with an electric guitar virtuoso on our worship team—or maybe we are the self-proclaimed virtuoso—but if our drummer is struggling to keep a 4/4 beat, then it really doesn't matter how amazing the electric guitar sounds. When it is played over a groove that is too difficult for our drummer to play well and the weakest link is pushed beyond their ability, the whole song will come crumbling down.

If, for example, the drummer is your weakest link, intentionally select songs they can play well. Make sure to utilize those songs frequently when that particular drummer is on the worship team—even if that is every week—so they can build on their previous work and not have to learn new songs every time. In this way, you will be building them up and helping them grow as a musician, all while serving the congregation with songs that are played well.

The same could be applied to every member of the worship team. We need to plan for the weakest link; we want to set people up for success, not failure.

Remember that we are called to play skillfully unto the Lord (see Psalm 33:3), but the Bible doesn't explicitly say what level of skill is necessary. I would suggest that playing skillfully means playing to the best of your ability. When musicians are asked to play too far above their skill level, it is neither loving to them nor helpful to the rest of the worship team or the congregation.

Give them a chance to play skillfully. Plan for the weakest link.

NOTES

EVERY SUNDAY LIKE A WEDDING

There is a time-honored wedding tradition in which the bride is supposed to bring to the wedding *something old, something new, something borrowed, something blue.* I like that. It reminds me of something Jesus once said:

> Every scribe who has been trained for the kingdom of heaven
> is like a master of a house, who brings out of his treasure what
> is new and what is old. (Matthew 13:52)

When we prepare to lead the church in Sunday morning worship, I believe it is beneficial to treat that moment like practice for the wedding that is to come. One day Christ will return for his bride, the church. Oh, what a day that will be! Until that day, we can practice.

As we continually practice for the wedding, I think it is appropriate for the bride (us) to bring, every Sunday, something old, something new, something borrowed, and something blue. What do I mean by that? I am referring to our song selection as worship leaders. How do you select your songs for each Sunday morning? Are you just using the songs that are most popular today? Do you depend heavily on older songs? Are you singing new, original, and unique songs to the Lord? Is there a place for lamentations in your song service?

Personally, I like the approach of treating each Sunday like a wedding. Practically speaking, this is what I mean:

Something Old: I always try to include a hymn in my Sunday morning set list. It is good to be reminded of the fact that the God we sing about today is the same God who has been sung about for generation after generation. We stand on the shoulders of giants when we sing songs about our faithful, never-changing God. Older members of the congregation will appreciate these songs, but it is not just for them. It is also (maybe especially) for the youth.

Something New: In saying "something new," I am referring to a song that is fresh, original, and unique to your specific congregation or context. It is biblical to sing a new song unto the Lord. (See Isaiah 42:10, Psalm 33:3, and Revelation 14:3, for example.) I always try to include a song that was written by myself or someone within the congregation or local community when I craft a Sunday morning set list.

Something Borrowed: The bulk of my Sunday morning set list falls into this category. In saying "something borrowed," I am referring to the current, most popular, and relevant church songs of today. The CCLI Top 100 is a great place to find songs to "borrow."

Something Blue: When you read through the Psalms, Israel's original songbook, you will notice there were many different expressions of worship for the people of Israel. One of those expressions was that of lamentation. The reality is that life is not always pleasant or fun. Sometimes life is tough. Sometimes life is noticeably not fair. If all we

EVERY SUNDAY LIKE A WEDDING

ever do on a Sunday morning is celebrate life's victories, we will alienate that large portion of our congregations that do not currently feel joyful or victorious. It is good and right to give a voice to their situation on a Sunday morning, as well. I always try to include something "blue" in my Sunday morning set list as a way of reminding one another that God is still good even when things are bad.

By applying the old adage and treating each Sunday like a wedding, you can be sure to have a well-rounded approach that will edify the largest number of people. In so doing, you will be like the scribe who has been trained for the kingdom of heaven as Jesus spoke of.

NOTES

OH NO, I MESSED UP!
WHAT NOW?

It happens to everyone. If it hasn't happened to you yet, or recently, it will. No one is exempt.

I was recently playing electric guitar for a local church worship team, and I totally messed up. We were playing a song that I had played a dozen times, and I landed on the wrong note of the signature electric guitar part. It was noticeable to anyone with ears. That note wasn't even pretending to be in the key. It was bad.

I messed up! What do I do now?

Obviously, the most important thing to do is to keep playing. Do your best. Try to shake it off. Keep your head up, keep calm, and finish strong. It can be hard to recover from such an obvious mistake, and I will admit that I played much more conservatively after letting that heinous note soar through the auditorium. I second-guessed myself from that point on and made a few additional (but less noticeable) mistakes as I attempted to finish strong.

I hate messing up. We all do. But here are some helpful tips for what to do after the inevitable takes place:

Take responsibility. Do not try to blame your mistake on someone else. Do not try to come up with excuses to save face. Not only is that approach dishonest and unloving, but you will not grow by using that method. In order to grow and improve, accept that you messed up.

Keep your head up. Personally, it is really easy to hang my head when I mess up. Part of that is probably shame. Part of it is pride. I hold myself to a high standard, and I really do not like failing to meet that standard. But the reality is that sometimes I don't meet my own standard. It's okay. Mistakes do not have to define who we are.

Sure, there will be those voices out there that are all too willing to remind you of your mess-ups, and sometimes that voice is our own. We have to choose to listen to the voice of God, who continually reminds us that our identity is not in what we can do but in what He has already done. Jesus died for us. The Father adopted us. The Holy Spirit is leading us. No silly little mistake will change that.

Get better. One of the fringe benefits of making a mistake is that it often helps to illuminate a weak spot. Maybe I didn't spend enough time practicing. Maybe I got distracted. Maybe there is a real, tangible reason why I made the mistake that I did. Keep in mind that I am not talking about making excuses, but about understanding what led to the mistake so that I don't repeat it in the future.

Extend grace to others. A second, powerful fringe benefit of making a mistake is that it should quicken our extension of grace to others when they mess up. We all make mistakes. No one is exempt. This time it was me. Next time it may be someone else. Hopefully, I will be as quick to show grace to others as I want them to be in showing grace to me.

NOTES

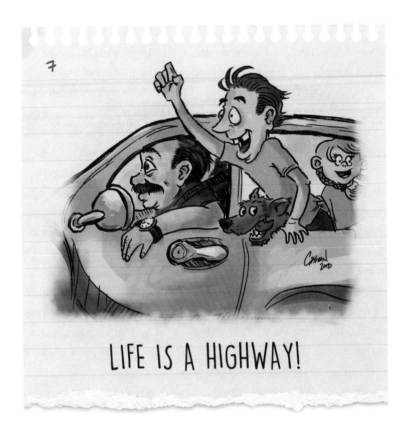

7

LIFE IS A HIGHWAY!

There is a song that came out during my childhood called, "Life Is A Highway." It was a great tune! Several artists have remade it since then, but I still remember that original version with the great drum beat, harmonica, and electric guitar in the opening, the almost-spoken first verse, and the classic chorus. "Life is a highway!"

While I don't necessarily ascribe to the entire worldview of the song, I think there are some helpful insights to offer to worship leaders as we look at life as a "highway."

Let's be honest; life has a lot of distractions! Kind of like billboards and signs and other vehicles on the road, life has a lot going on. It can be hard to stay focused with so many distractions vying for our attention. As worshipers, we can certainly become distracted ourselves, but as worship leaders, we must recognize this constant pull that our people face and try to help them stay focused in the midst of the distraction. Many times while traveling on a highway with my GPS (Global Positioning System), I will hear it say something like, "Merge left in one mile," and I realize that I have totally forgotten what I was doing. I was just going through the motions. That friendly little reminder from my GPS redirects my focus and helps me engage again. As worship leaders, it can be helpful for us to look for ways to act as sort of a GPS (God Positioning System). We are not standing up front just to perform or to simply lead songs. Life is a highway! People get distracted. It is a good idea to remind people of what we are doing, even while we are doing it, to help redirect their focus and get them ready to engage again.

Sometimes I travel through the night. I enjoy doing that because there is hardly anyone else on the highway and I can cover a lot of ground. It is supremely important for us, as worship leaders, to do a fair amount of "night driving." By that, I mean that we need to spend a significant amount of time in our prayer closet, being alone with the Father. Jesus, the Ultimate Worship Leader, often withdrew to lonely places to pray. (See Luke 5:16.) We should, too! We are doing a huge disservice to our people and ourselves if our main prayer time is on stage, in front of others. Life is a highway! Get out there and do some lonely night driving.

With the exception of some night driving, most of our time spent on the highway will be in the midst of others. The highway is filled with other drivers. They have their own agenda, their own schedule, and their own thoughts of how the driving should be done. We may all be moving smoothly towards our destination, or we may wind up in a bit of a traffic jam. There may even be tragic moments when two or more cars collide, creating minor or devastating damage. Though this should be avoided as much as possible, it is a part of life. Life is a highway! Always be mindful of those around you. As a worship leader, be aware that your actions can help others move smoothly towards their heavenly destination or have devastating consequences.

So many of the highway travelers have entered at different points. Creating as many on-ramps as possible allows for as many travelers as possible. As worship leaders, we need to realize that some people are ready to enter into worship as soon as they walk through the church doors, while others are ready at the start of the first song. Still others may not be ready to enter until much later into the set list, if at all. No worries! Just acknowledge this reality and offer as many on-ramps as possible.

One way I like to do this is by saying a few words between each song to help people understand why we are singing it. I explain why I chose it, how it fits Biblically or thematically to the morning service, or what it means to me on a personal level. I also tend to speak the words of the next line of the song prior to singing it. This method serves as sort of an "on-ramp." I know that, typically, the lyrics are displayed on the screen behind me, but this simple gesture helps communicate that I want people to sing along and that they don't have to stare at the screen. They can close their eyes and focus on God, and I will occasionally be feeding them lyrics. On a practical side, it also helps the person running the overhead projection to know for sure where I am going, clearing up possible distractions.

NOTES

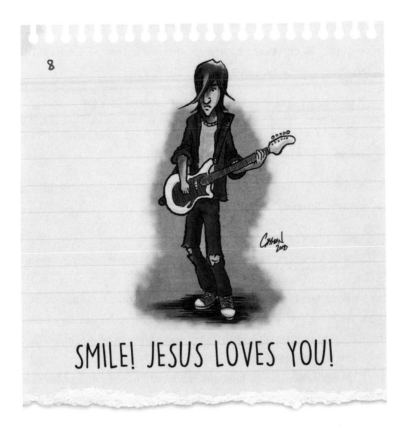

8

SMILE! JESUS LOVES YOU!

Smile! Jesus loves you!

Several years ago, my wife and I visited a large, prominent church that is known throughout the country for their excellence in preaching, and also for delivering great, accessible songs to the North American church. I was so excited to go!

What a letdown.

That morning taught me something I will never forget. It wasn't the words spoken by the pastor from the pulpit. It wasn't anything the worship leader said. In fact, it was something they DIDN'T do. They didn't smile.

To be clear, the music was excellent and the preaching was commendable. The facilities, volunteers, and programming were as professional as any that I have encountered before or since. But it all left me feeling a bit empty. They didn't smile!

A glad heart makes a cheerful face. (Proverbs 15:13a)

The light of the eyes rejoices the heart, and good news refreshes the bones. (Proverbs 15:30)

Rejoice in hope, be patient in tribulation, be constant in prayer. (Romans 12:12)

Smile! Jesus loves you!

Worship leaders, it is weird to sing about the matchless love of Christ, the good news of the gospel, and the hope that we have in Jesus without being excited about what we are singing. If we are excited about what we are singing, then we really ought to let our face know about it! That is, after all, our primary way of letting others know that we are excited about it.

I am not interested in fake. No one wants to see fake smiles that communicate I-am-smiling-right-now-because-I-know-that-I-have-to... No. Please, just no. But if we can catch even a glimpse of the incredible truth that we get to lead people in singing about week after week, it really ought to gladden our heart and result in bearing a cheerful face.

This good news, when taken to heart, will light up our eyes and refresh our bones. We have so much hope to rejoice in.

No, I am not interested in fake. But to be honest, the message being communicated that morning came across as fake precisely BECAUSE it wasn't delivered with a smile. I was not convinced that they really believed what they were singing and speaking about.

I know that the tendency—and the temptation—is to be cool. Trust me, the worship leader and the pastor at this church were both really cool! They had perfect hair. They were perfectly (relevantly) dressed. They spoke clearly and precisely. The service was perfectly put together.

I was impressed, but I wasn't impressed by God. I wasn't impressed by the work that He had clearly done in the hearts of these leaders. I actually left that morning wondering if they even knew the God they sang and spoke about so perfectly. Did they know He came to give us abundant life? Did they know He wants our joy to be full? Did they know He loves us so much that He sent His only Son to die for us? Do you? If you do, don't forget to let your face know about it. Smile! Jesus loves you!

NOTES

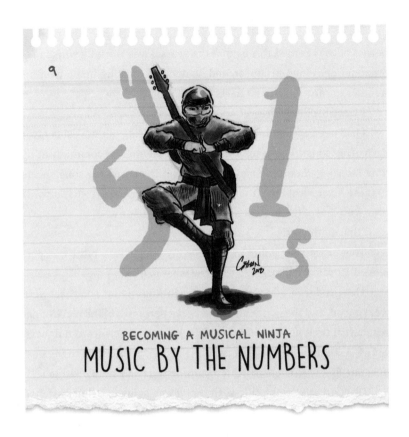

BECOMING A MUSICAL NINJA
MUSIC BY THE NUMBERS

When I was a kid, I was amazed by my dad's driving skills. I was old enough to understand the basic idea of how to get from point A to point B, no problem. But somehow he always knew a faster way to get there. It was like he was some kind of car ninja—or perhaps a road wizard who understood the mystic arts of cartography at a level that mere mortals could never attain.

How was he doing that? Did he possess some sort of sixth sense? What was the secret to his navigational success?

It wasn't until I was much older that I witnessed this same level of superior knowledge being utilized not for travel, but for music.

I was twenty-five years old when I first recorded in a professional studio in Nashville, TN. This was a studio where many of my musical heroes have recorded throughout the years. I was working with a professional, seasoned producer, and he decided to bring in a few of his buddies to record different parts for the project.

I was absolutely in awe!

I had been accustomed to meticulously writing out song sheets for each of my songs. Those song sheets were essential for communicating how the song should be played. I awkwardly offered my song sheets to these masters of their trade, who had just finished up a nationwide tour with one of the biggest artists in Christian music.

"Um, no thanks!"

They were very polite in refusing my song sheet, but I was perplexed. How were they going to know what to play?

The producer played back the recording of the song we were working on, and the guitar guru grabbed a pen and a blank piece of paper. In real time, as the song played, he started jotting down numbers. 1, 1, 4, 5. Then he went to the next line. 1, 1, 4, 5. And then to the next line. 6m, 6m, 4, 5. Then he went to another line and simply wrote a 1.

He continued doing this as the song was playing. He just listened in real time and wrote seemingly random numbers on the paper. After the song played through once, he said, "Let's do it."

Placing the paper with the jumbled mess of numbers on a music stand, he picked up his guitar and flawlessly played my song as if he had been playing it all of his life.

Wait, what is this dark magic?! How did he do this? How did he access this incredible shortcut?

Simple. He was using what is commonly referred to as the "Nashville Numbers System" (NNS). This systematic approach to playing music applies universal principles of contemporary western music and translates them into simple ways of quickly and effectively communicating them to the whole team of musicians. By applying a basic understanding of music theory, all of the important information, such as beats, chords, and progressions (and more) can be easily transferred and/or transposed, as needed.

In the following chapters, I will be unpacking a basic understanding of music theory to help worship teams practically utilize the NNS. Then we can all be musical ninjas, wizards, and gurus as we work together to lead God's people in musical worship.

NOTES

10

BECOMING A MUSICAL NINJA
WE GOT THE BEAT!

Let's get super practical! Music is the combination of tones, frequencies, chords, and progressions played together over a set amount of time. That set amount of time is called the "beat." As we unpack the Nashville Numbers System, it will not make any sense without a basic understanding of musical beat.

The vast majority of contemporary western music uses four beats in each measure. Simply put, that means the basic musical phrase or feel repeats itself every four beats. For these songs, you could count "one, two, three, four," along with the beat, and you would likely hear chord changes on the "one." Again, this is by far the most commonly used time signature in contemporary western music, but it is certainly not the only one. This time signature is called **"4/4"** because there are four beats for each measure.

A classic example of a song written in 4/4 is "Hark! the Herald Angels Sing." If you count it out, the measure starts over again on *hark, angels, glory,* and *newborn.* Those words sit on the first beat of each measure, or the "one" beat.

Some songs have three beats to a measure, which means that you count them as, "one, two, three," and then start a new measure. This time signature is called **"3/4"** because there are three beats for each measure. A classic example of a song written in 3/4 is "The First Noel." If you count it out, the measure starts over again on *first, el, angels,* and *say.* Take into consideration that the song starts on a pickup beat before that first measure we counted and that the *el* is the second syllable of the word *Noel.*

Contemporary western music will also use **2/4** and **6/8,** as well as many other rarely used time signatures. If the song works better to count two beats to a measure (instead of 4/4), or six beats to a measure (instead of 3/4), then the song is actually written in 2/4 or 6/8, respectively.

Using the most common time signature, which is overwhelmingly 4/4, let's look at the most common ways to fill the measure.

If you are counting "one, two, three, four," for the beats of a 4/4 song, then you are counting **quarter notes.** A quarter note is a note that is played for one quarter of a 4/4 measure, or one beat. It is important to point out that the quarter note is still just one beat in any other time signature, even though that would technically be half of a 2/4 measure.

A **half note,** then, is half of the 4/4 measure, or two beats. A **whole note** would be held out for the duration of the entire measure, or four beats.

Going in the other direction, notes can actually occupy less than one beat. An **eighth note** is half of a beat. To count eighth notes, you count the measure as, "one and two and three and four." Each word represents an eighth note.

Although much more could be said about this and about the many ways to fill—and go beyond—a measure, we will, for our purposes here, go no further than acknowledging the **sixteenth note**, which is a quarter of a beat. You can fit four sixteenth notes into a single beat, and sixteen sixteenth notes into a single measure, and you count that measure as, "one e and ah, two e and ah, three e and ah, four e and ah." Again, each word (or something like a word) represents a sixteenth note.

Those are the basics of the musical beat. Once you've got the beat, you want to know how quickly those beats are moving. The tempo of a song is determined by **"Beats Per Minute,"** or **"BPM."** Once you have your time signature and tempo, you are ready to talk about the key.

	1	2	3	4	2	2	3	4
WHOLE NOTE	𝅝				𝅝			
HALF NOTE	𝅗𝅥		𝅗𝅥		𝅗𝅥		𝅗𝅥	
QUARTER NOTE	♩	♩	♩	♩	♩	♩	♩	♩
EIGHTH NOTE	♫	♫	♫	♫	♫	♫	♫	♫
SIXTEENTH NOTE	♬♬	♬♬	♬♬	♬♬	♬♬	♬♬	♬♬	♬♬

NOTES

11

BECOMING A MUSICAL NINJA
THE KEEPER OF THE KEYS

When I first started writing songs, I literally pulled out my origami skills and created a couple of cubes that would become my "chord dice." I wrote every chord that I knew on the pair of dice, and I rolled the dice to decide what chord I would play. One of those two chords, I figured, would have to sound good!

I'm not joking; that's a true story. It did NOT sound good. I had no idea what I was doing.

Songwriting, to me, was some sort of magical, mystical métier. One had to be an outright master of their craft in order to put the notes and chords in the correct order. With so many possible combinations, how could anyone ever know anything about the mysterious nature of music?

As I continued to learn and dig deeper into the subject, I soon realized that music is actually not very difficult.

In contemporary western music, songs are typically written in a specific key and only include notes and chords that are a part of that key. In fact, each song essentially uses seven notes over and over again.

Seven... now that's not such a difficult number. But before we talk about seven, let's go a little higher and talk about twelve.

There are essentially twelve notes in contemporary western music. Those twelve notes, then, just repeat themselves over and over, using higher and lower frequencies of the same basic notes. The eighty-eight keys of a piano are just these same twelve notes being used over and over again, but using a higher frequency version of those same notes from left to right. Those twelve basic notes are:

A, A# (or Bb), B, C, C# (or Db), D, D# (or Eb), E, F, F# (or Gb), G, G# (or Ab)

You may have noticed that some notes have two names. The hashtag indicates that the note is **sharp**, or one half step higher than the note beside it. The little "b" indicates that the note is **flat**, or one half step lower than the note beside it.

There, that was easy. Right? So where does that "seven" number come into play? Each key contains only seven of these twelve possible notes. The seven notes are set for each key, and songs rarely use notes outside of the song key.

So how do you know which seven notes will be in the key that the song is using? There is actually a simple formula. It goes like this: Root, whole, whole, half, whole, whole, whole, half. (The key actually includes eight notes, but the eighth note is always a repeat of the first note. That repeat is called the **octave** of the root note.)

R, w, w, h, w, w, w, h

Start with the key in which the song is written. We'll use the key of A as an example. The note directly to the right of A is a **half step** away from A. Two half steps make a **whole step**. So following the simple formula, the key of A would include the following seven notes:

Root: **A**, whole: **B**, whole: **C#**, half: **D**, whole: **E**, whole: **F#**, whole: **G#**, half: **A**.

Well, look at that! We effectively erased five possible notes from the song. This formula works for any key. Let's try the key of C:

Root: **C**, whole: **D**, whole: **E**, half: **F**, whole: **G**, whole: **A**, whole: **B**, half: **C**.

Once you have a grasp of which notes are a part of the key, you are well on your way to becoming a musical wizard.

NOTES

12

BECOMING A MUSICAL NINJA
MAJOR MINORS

It's time to get super practical! Once you understand how to formulate the likely possible notes for any given key (seven possible notes), we can take those seven numbers down to the most likely four chords.

Four chords. Anyone can memorize four chords, right?

Honestly, most contemporary western music only uses four chords in a given song. There are many exceptions to this, of course, but you may be surprised to find out how many times it is true.

So how do you know which four chords will be the "magic four"? It's actually quite simple. Let's take our formula for finding the notes in a given key (R, w, w, h, w, w, w, h), and ascribe numbers to each step of the formula. It would look like this:

R (**1**), w (**2**), w (**3**), h (**4**), w (**5**), w (**6**), w (**7**), h (**8**)

Now let's keep it practical by using an actual key. For example, let's use the key of G:

R: **G** (**1**), w: **A** (**2**), w: **B** (**3**), h: **C** (**4**), w: **D** (**5**), w: **E** (**6**), w: **F#** (**7**), h: **G** (**8**)

We have officially converted the key of G into numbers. Now we are getting somewhere!

Although the formula we were using (R, w, w, h, w, w, w, h) is meant to help us find what **notes** are in a given key, it is also telling us what **chords** are in a given key... kind of. We still have one thing to take into consideration. There are typical **major** chord numbers and typical **minor** chord numbers.

1, 4, and 5 are major chord numbers. 2, 3, and 6 are minor chord numbers. This means that in the key of G, for example, the typical chords that are used will be:

G (1), **Am** (2), **Bm** (3), **C** (4), **D** (5), **Em** (6), **F#dim** (7), **G** (8)

You may have noticed that the seven chord was neither major nor minor. It is actually diminished. No worries; the seven chord is rarely ever used as a full chord. It is typically only used as a note that is added as a bass note to the five chord.

Knowing the majors and minors for a given key is very helpful, but we still haven't discovered our "magic four" chords. You remember, right? Those magic four chords that make up the vast majority of all contemporary western songs? Well here they are:

1, 4, 5, and 6.

These are, without a doubt, the most popular chords in any song. If you were to memorize the 1, 4, 5, and 6 chord of every key, you could play pretty much any song on the radio.

What's more, once you get this reality in your mind, you can actually hear the chord changes in a given song and know, just by hearing, which chord is being played. The 1 chord will always feel like home. It just feels right, resolved. The 4 chord is a lift, but there is a bit of tension with it. It is not lifted as high as it could be. The 5 chord lifts as far from home as you would want to stray. The 6 minor, though it lifts higher yet, actually feels lower, more mysterious, and full of tension.

Try listening to songs to see if you can spot the 1, 4, 5, and 6. As a hint, it may help to know that throughout time, the most popular chord progression has been 1 5 6 4.

NOTES

13

BECOMING A MUSICAL NINJA

WHERE DO CHORDS COME FROM?

There is an interesting legend that has come to us by way of European folklore in which it is said that newborn babies are delivered by way of a stork. Perhaps you have heard of the legend. Perhaps you once believed the legend (or maybe you still do).

It is a ridiculous notion, of course. Newborn babies are definitely not carried by a stork and gracefully dropped into the laps of hopeful, expectant mothers. I never believed that story. However, had you told me that a stork carried music chords and gracefully dropped them into the laps of hopeful, expectant musicians and songwriters, I probably would have believed you!

What is the deal with chords, anyway? Where do they come from?

When I was much younger, I used to place my fingers randomly on the fretboard of a guitar or haphazardly on the family piano and just hope against hope that my fingers had magically discovered a chord. Nope. Whatever terrible sound I had concocted, it was definitely not a chord, or at least not a chord that anyone musical would ever consider using in a song. I was dumbfounded. Where exactly did chords come from?

I later found out exactly where chords come from, and I want to share that knowledge with you. First, though, I should warn you: this is a very simple explanation of chordal theory, and much more could be said on the subject. Because the vast majority of contemporary western music uses only the notes within the key of the song, I will stick to explaining typical major and minor chords within a given key. Let's recap what we already know:

There are twelve possible notes for any given key:

A, A# (or Bb), B, C, C# (or Db), D, D# (or Eb), E, F, F# (or Gb), G, G# (or Ab)

But there are actually only seven notes in a given key, with the eight note being a repeat of the first. You can figure out what seven notes are in a key by using the following formula:

Root, whole, whole, half, whole, whole, whole, half

That formula also tells you which number each chord will represent:

R (1), w (2), w (3), h (4), w (5), w (6), w (7), h (8)

We also know that the 1, 4, and 5 are major chords and the 2, 3, and 6 are minor chords. (The seven is diminished and we will not worry about it for now, as it is typically only added as a bass note to the five chord.)

With all of that information in mind, we are ready to understand where chords come from. It's simple, really. Using the major scale formula (R, w, w, h, w, w, w, h), we find major chords by using the 1, 3, and 5 of the chord's major scale. An E chord, for instance, uses the 1, 3, and 5 of the E major scale. The notes in the E major scale are:

E (1), **F#** (2), **G#** (3), **A** (4), **B** (5), **C#** (6), **D#** (7), **E** (8)

Therefore, the notes in the E chord are:

E (1), **G#** (3), and **B** (5)

This formula works for any major chord in any key. However, it is important to point out that to find the notes in a chord, you have to use the major scale of the chord you are trying to find, and not the major scale of the key of the song. For instance, the four chord in the key of E is the A chord. To find the notes in the A chord, you have to use the 1, 3, and 5 of the A major scale, which is:

A (1), **B** (2), **C#** (3), **D** (4), **E** (5), **F#** (6), **G#** (7), **A** (8)

Therefore, the notes in the A chord are:

A (1), **C#** (3), and **E** (5)

To discover the notes within a **minor chord**, you use a similar formula, but you go one half step down from the third note of the chord's major scale. In the key of E, the six chord would be minor. Let's find the notes within the **C#m chord** by locating the 1, 3b, and 5 of the C# major scale, which is:

C# (1), **D#** (2), **E#** (3), **F#** (4), **G#** (5), **A#** (6), **B#** (7), **C#** (8)

Don't forget that the third note in the scale has to be flattened, or dropped one half step lower in order to create a minor chord. So the notes that make up the C#m chord are:

NOTE

TO BE WRITTEN CORRECTLY, THE MAJOR SCALE NEEDS TO INCLUDE ALL SEVEN LETTERS; THEREFORE, WHEN WRITING OUT THE C# MAJOR SCALE, YOU WOULD USE THE NOTE E# INSTEAD OF F AND B# INSTEAD OF C.

C# (1), **E** (3b), and **G#** (5)

One final secret: every note within every chord of a given key should also be within the scale of the key of the song itself. Notice that the E major chord used the notes **E**, **G#**, and **B**. The A major chord used the notes **A**, **C#**, and **E**. The C# minor chord used the notes **C#**, **E**, and **G#**. All of those notes are within the E major scale. In fact, a simpler way to find the notes within a chord (within a major scale) would be to start with the number of the chord itself, skip a number, and use the next chord.

So...

The **1** chord of a major scale would use that scale's **1, 3,** and **5** notes to create a chord.

The **2** chord of a major scale would use that scale's **2, 4,** and **6** notes to create a chord.

The **3** chord of a major scale would use that scale's **3, 5,** and **7** notes to create a chord.

The **4** chord of a major scale would use that scale's **4, 6,** and **1** notes to create a chord.

The **5** chord of a major scale would use that scale's **5, 7,** and **2** notes to create a chord.

The **6** chord of a major scale would use that scale's **6, 1,** and **3** notes to create a chord.

The **7** chord of a major scale would use that scale's **7, 2,** and **4** notes to create a chord.

Sorry, no storks. But hopefully, this information helps explain exactly where those pesky chords come from, and how to create them on any instrument.

| | C | D | E | F | G | A | B | C |
	1	2	3	4	5	6	7	8
I CHORD	C		E		G			
2 CHORD		D		F		A		
3 CHORD			E		G		B	
4 CHORD				F		A		C
5 CHORD		D			G		B	
6 CHORD			E			A		C
7 CHORD		D		F			B	

NOTES

14

BECOMING A MUSICAL NINJA
PUTTING IT ALL TOGETHER

In the last several chapters, we have talked about becoming a musical ninja. We outlined the different parameters for musical beat, discovered how to know what notes and chords are in each key, how those chords within a key can be represented by numbers, and even what notes make up each individual chord.

We learned a lot!

With great knowledge comes great responsibility. So... what now? What do we do with all of this knowledge? Why does it matter? How is it going to be helpful to us? Most importantly, how will this knowledge transform us into musical ninjas?

We have to put all this information together in order to understand and utilize the Nashville Numbers System. Let's start with an easy key: C

Our twelve possible notes for the key are:

A, A# (or **Bb**), B, C, C# (or **Db**), D, D# (or **Eb**), E, F, F# (or **Gb**), G, G# (or **Ab**)

In any given key, you will either use sharps or flats, but not both. The key of C, however, has no sharps or flats at all. That is why it is an easy key. Starting with C as our root note, and using our major scale formula (or, in this case, simply using our knowledge that the key of C has no sharps or flats and that each letter has to be represented in the scale), we can quickly find the notes in our scale:

Root: **C**, whole: **D**, whole: **E**, half: **F**, whole: **G**, whole: **A**, whole: **B**, half: **C**

Now let's give each of those notes a corresponding number:

C (1), **D** (2), **E** (3), **F** (4), **G** (5), **A** (6), **B** (7), **C** (8)

And let's remember that the 1, 4, and 5 are major chord numbers, while the 2, 3, and 6 are minor chord numbers. The seven is diminished and is rarely ever used in typical western music, but we'll include it in our scale, anyway. Therefore, the chords available to us in the key of C will be:

C (1), **Dm** (2), **Em** (3), **F** (4), **G** (5), **Am** (6), **Bdim** (7), C (8)

Our four magic chords are the 1, 4, 5, and 6 (**C, F, G,** and **Am**), and the most likely chord progression would be 1 5 6 4 (**C G Am F**).

Let's write that progression using the Nashville Numbers System. Let's assume the song is written in 4/4, and each chord lasts for four beats (or one whole note). Written in NNS, that chord progression would look like this:

1 5 6 4

Now, if you happened to play that progression and were overcome with an undeniable urge to sing "Blessed Be Your Name," "Give Us Clean Hands," "Hallelujah (Your Love Makes Me Sing)," "Here I Am to Worship," or "The Heart of Worship," it's okay! There is nothing wrong with you (other than the fact that you may have grown up in the late eighties or early nineties). All of those songs (and many, many more) used the 1 5 6 4 progression in their chorus.

The beautiful thing about the Nashville Numbers System is that it makes changing keys a simple task. 1 5 6 4 in the key of C is still 1 5 6 4 in the key of G, except now the chords are **G D Em C.**

NOTES

TOOLS OF THE TRADE

Imagine I told you that some guy built my house without using a tape measure. Would you believe me? I hope not. Either that is not a true story, or my house is VERY noticeable.

A good builder would never attempt to build something of significance, like a house, without having some standard tool for measuring. As ridiculous as it sounds for one man to build a house without a tape measure (and it does!), now imagine a whole crew of builders working on that same house without relying on the standard, accurate, and agreed-upon measurement of a tape measure. We all know that this scenario would not end well. With everyone just "eyeballing" it, the house would be a mess!

Now imagine that I told you some worship team led worship music without using a metronome. Would you believe me? Yes, you probably would.

For some unknown reason, we have been fooled into believing that a metronome is something that only "beginners" or "crazy old piano teachers" use. No! That is not true! It may surprise you to know that professional musicians use a metronome pretty much all of the time.

A metronome is used when writing a song to make sure all of the expressions fit into the same basic time parameters. Without it, verses, choruses, bridges, and interludes may develop their own individual feel and be disjointed when they come together as one song. One of the first things I do when writing a song is to decide what BPM (beats per minute) best fit the melody or chord progression with which I am working. While I may make adjustments to the overall BPM as I continue to write, the metronome is an important part of the process.

A metronome is used when practicing a song. I like to make sure the entire worship team knows what BPM we will be using for each song. This can be accomplished by simply including the tempo information on the song sheet. Knowing the BPM is nearly as important as knowing the key for each song. I always try to practice in the right key and with the correct tempo. If everyone on the worship team is doing this during their personal practice time, the song will come together naturally when we rehearse as a team.

A metronome is used when recording a song. Every time I set up a recording session, I first enter the BPM of the song. In fact, I often do this even before I enter the key for the song, although that part is important, as well. During the recording process, musicians do not always record at the same time. Often, days or even weeks will go by between recording one instrument and then another. The only way to hold the song together is with a metronome (often called a "click track" in the recording world) that each musician listens to while they are recording their part. Since each musician is using the same standard, accurate, and agreed-upon measurement, each individual part will fit perfectly into the whole. **A metronome can even be used when playing live.** Personally, I prefer this, as does nearly every professional touring musician. While using a metronome for playing live is not always possible in a church setting, a few small adjustments can get you on the road to better timing. Consistent personal practice with a metronome will increase the overall feel and timing of each musician, even if it is not used live. Plugging a metronome into the system and letting it come through the floor monitors during rehearsal is a simple way to improve the overall feel and timing of the worship team as a group. If your worship team uses IEM (In Ear Monitors), you can have the metronome running during both the rehearsal and the service without it becoming a distraction to the congregation.

The metronome is one of the simplest, most helpful, and often most underutilized tools of the trade for musicians. A builder would never attempt to build a house without a tape measure in their tool belt, and musicians should never attempt to build a musical worship set without the consistent use of a metronome.

NOTES

16

MUSICIANS FROM MARS, VOCALISTS FROM VENUS

There was a book published during my childhood called, *Men are from Mars, Women are from Venus.* I never read the book; I think I was twelve when it was first released. While I am sure it was a great book, my hunch is that it was written with a simple premise in mind: *men and women are different.* Men and women act differently, have different tendencies, and even speak different languages (in a sense). Their differences are so great that it's almost as though they come from two different planets.

I think that idea is helpful. I also think it could be beneficial to us as worship leaders. To be clear, though, I am not talking here about the difference between men and women. I am talking about the difference between Musicians and Vocalists. Musicians are from Mars, Vocalists are from Venus.

For years I operated as a worship leader who did not quite understand this dynamic. I could sense it in my gut, but I didn't have the clarity to actually name it and act accordingly.

Practically speaking, I would conduct worship team rehearsals with both species (Musicians *and* Vocalists) on the stage. I assumed this was what everybody did. In fact, it probably *was* what everybody did. But it was a source of constant frustration.

At certain points of the rehearsal, I would stop to talk with the electric guitarist about a certain part. The Vocalists must have heard me speaking in another language, perhaps *Musicianese,* and they assumed it was a great time to start talking with one another... in their mother tongue of *Vocalish*... into the mic. Not cool.

Of course, at other points of the rehearsal, I would stop to talk with the Vocalists about a particular word or phrase or harmony idea. The Musicians must have heard me speaking in Vocalish, and took it as an opportunity to work on their musical chops. While trying to speak with the Vocalists, I would hear the electric guitar solo, the opening drum roll, a piano scale, or the bridge chord progression for the acoustic guitar... all being played... at the same time... through the system. Not cool.

Why did this happen? I believe that it happened primarily because Musicians are from Mars and Vocalists are from Venus.

Yes, I could have demanded everyone's attention and lectured about how rude it was for the Vocalists to talk amongst themselves while I was helping the Musicians, or for the Musicians to play the instrument at their fingertips while I was talking with the Vocalists. But honestly, I was going to have the same conversation in ten minutes... and next week... and the week after that.

There is a better way! After years of trying to figure out how to most effectively navigate through the dynamic differences of Musicians and Vocalists, I realized that it was best to just split them up.

I asked one of my best Vocalists if they would be willing to lead the Vocalists through the songs in another room for the first forty-five minutes of our rehearsal. During those forty-five minutes, they would listen to the songs together, work on harmonies, learn the words, and speak all of the Vocalish their hearts desired. Meanwhile, I was in the sanctuary working with the Musicians. During those same forty-five minutes, we would work through the songs, talk through parts and progressions, and speak to one another in Musicianese without alienating our Vocal counterparts.

After that first forty-five-minute segment, we would come together for a fifteen-minute devotional/prayer time, and then spend thirty minutes rehearsing the songs with Musicians and Vocalists on stage as if it were Sunday morning. This strategy worked so well, you could say it was out of this world!

NOTES

17

A LITTLE BIT OF STARBUCKS GOES A LONG WAY

I do not believe that worship team members should ever need to be thanked for their service. Seriously. I don't. Having the privilege of leading God's people into an awareness of His presence and glory should be more than enough satisfaction for anyone.

I resonate with the Psalmist who considered simply being in the courts of God to be better than anything else.

> For a day in your courts is better than a thousand elsewhere.
> I would rather be a doorkeeper in the house of my God than
> dwell in the tents of wickedness. (Psalm 84:10)

Not only should being in God's presence and leading God's people into musical worship be satisfying to our souls, but our security in who we are should be found in Whose we are. We are His! Why would we need the praise of man when we have the presence of God, our Father? He is our Rock and our Refuge! Our security is found in Him alone, and it is more than sufficient.

I do not believe that worship team members should ever need to be thanked for their service.

But why not do it, anyway?

It is biblical to find your satisfaction in God alone, but it is also biblical to encourage one another:

> But encourage one another daily, as long as it is called "Today," so that none of you may be hardened by sin's deceitfulness. (Hebrews 3:13, NIV)

> Encourage one another and build one another up.
> (1 Thessalonians 5:11a)

The reality is that our worship team members spend hours of practice and preparation each week so that they can bring a skillful contribution to the musical worship. Hopefully, they do this out of a motive to serve the worship leader, the congregation, and ultimately, God. That is pretty commendable, wouldn't you say?

While I don't believe that worship team members should ever need to be thanked, I think it is a good practice to look for ways to bless them, anyway.

There are a myriad of simple ways to do this. Here are a few suggestions:

Tell them you appreciate them. Nothing communicates, "I appreciate you," quite like the words, "I appreciate you." If you haven't told your team members that in a while, you're probably way overdue.

Send them a note. In this day of marvelous technological advancements, it is quite easy to send a quick email or text (or multiple other methods of messaging) to your team members to encourage them.

Buy them a coffee. Admittedly, this one is my personal favorite. (But then again, coffee is my love language.) On the way to rehearsal, consider picking up an extra java (or nine), and treat the team to some piping hot liquid love. If it is not practical to stop by on your way, or if you don't think that coffee would be allowed in your rehearsal space, consider giving $5 gift cards as a token of your appreciation. Believe me, a little bit of Starbucks goes a long way!

NOTES

THE SOUND MAN IS YOUR FRIEND

Between 1455 and 1487, there was a civil war that plagued the land of England. Historically known as the "Wars of the Roses," two royal households from the same lineage fought as bitter enemies for more than thirty years! The House of Lancaster, whose family banner sported a red rose, and the House of York, whose family banner sported a white rose, brutally battled one another for the undisputed claim to the throne. Ultimately, the House of Lancaster won the war, but then the king married Elizabeth from the House of York, thereby reuniting the two families.

What a pointless battle!

Too many times I have seen this same "War of the Roses" play out in a church worship team setting. Often there is a battle between the

House of Worship Leader and the House of Audio Department for the undisputed claim to the throne. This is a pointless battle!

Worship leaders, I have important information for you. Please read carefully.

The sound man is your friend. When I travel around training worship teams, this is a phrase I often have them memorize and repeat: "The sound man is my friend."

You are on the same team. We don't always think of the sound man (or sound woman) as being a part of the worship team, but they are. In fact, they are a vital part of the worship team. Like the Houses of Lancaster and York, we can easily slip into a pointless power struggle. Maybe the sound man is secretly turning things down in the stage monitors so that he can provide a better front-of-house mix, or maybe the electric guitar player is covertly boosting the volume of his amplifier on the stage. This unhealthy and unhelpful mix battle never ends well. The sound man is your friend. You should be working together to create a stage volume and front-of-house volume that serves the congregation as well as the worship team.

The sound man can make you or break you. As a worship leader, you could be standing in front of the congregation making the most spiritually enlightened point on this side of eternity, but if your mic is muted, no one will hear it. You could be singing notes that compel even the angels of heaven to sing along, but if your vocal is buried in the mix (or if it is way too loud), then your melodious invitation to make much of God will be missed. On the flip side, if you accidentally put your capo on the wrong fret or if the keyboard is transposed into the wrong key, a quick-witted sound man can heroically save the day with a single fader. The reality is that the sound man has the ability to enhance the mix, fix the mix, or destroy the mix. It is far better to befriend someone with this much power than it is to merely hope he is on your side.

The sound man has a thankless job. He already knows that. The congregation typically only notices the sound man when something goes terribly wrong. Ironically, in times of sonic disaster, he will most likely be blamed whether it was his fault or yours. When everything is going well, probably no one will realize or acknowledge how much he contributed to the success of the service.

The sound man could use your help. Believe it or not, your sound man likely wants to serve you well. While it is ultimately his hands on the board, he would probably respond well to hearing you express how you would like different aspects of the music to sound. If there is a specific guitar part you would like to have louder, let him know. If there is a specific effect you would like for him to use at a particular moment in the song, tell him. You can accomplish much more musically by working together than you ever can on your own.

So please remember: the sound man is your friend!

NOTES

WE ARE GATHERED TOGETHER...
TO BE ALONE?

There is one contemporary worship phenomenon that just has to stop. Please. Just stop.

I am always amazed when worship leaders say something from the stage to the effect of, "This time is just for you and God..." Or, "Everyone close your eyes, forget about the people next to you, and just focus on Jesus..."

Um... what?!

This approach to corporate worship is, like, basically the complete opposite of what corporate worship is all about!

Here is an interesting thought: You don't have to be at church to worship God. In fact, I believe that Jesus gave us a bit of insight into what God-honoring personal worship looks like.

When you pray, go into your room and shut the door and pray
to your Father who is in secret. And your Father who sees in
secret will reward you. (Matthew 6:6)

This is really great advice! As worshipers, we are called to spend
quality time alone with God. It is good to set aside time to just be with
Him. It can be helpful to close our eyes and focus on Jesus, but not
during corporate worship.

"Corporate" means "group." The word comes from the idea of
many people becoming as one body. This is what happens when the
church comes together to worship God corporately. All of us, mindful
of one another, worship our Father together as one body.

I love the "us" and "our" language that is used throughout the
Psalms:

O Lord, **our** Lord, how majestic is your name in all the earth!
You have set your glory above the heavens. (Psalm 8:1, emphasis added)

Lord, you have been **our** dwelling place in all generations.
(Psalm 90:1, emphasis added)

Oh come, let **us** sing to the LORD; let us make a joyful noise to
the rock of **our** salvation! (Psalm 95:1, emphasis added)

This idea gets picked up and solidified by Paul in the New Testament, as well:

What then, brothers? When you come together, each one has
a hymn, a lesson, a revelation, a tongue, or an interpretation.
Let all things be done for building up. (1 Corinthians 14:26)

Worship leaders, there is a time for everything. Yes, there absolutely is a time for our people to be alone with God, but that time is not
during corporate worship.

When we come together, we come to worship God together. Do not encourage your people to close their eyes and forget about their neighbors! (And don't do it yourself, either!) Rather, encourage your people to open their eyes and realize they are not alone in this journey of pursuing God.

We are gathered together... to be together. Let's embrace this truth. Let's celebrate this truth! Our corporate worship times serve as the one—and probably the only—time of the week that our people have to worship our Father together, corporately, many people as one body.

NOTES

20

COME HUNGRY,
BUT NOT STARVED

There is something absolutely beautiful about the church coming together to worship God on a regular basis. I say "regular" because most churches that I am familiar with meet weekly, but I have visited many churches overseas that meet on a daily basis. I am even aware of churches that meet every other week. I am not sure that the actual amount of time between meetings is nearly as important as the fact that it is an agreed upon, clearly communicated, and regular coming together of the body of Christ.

The Holy Spirit-inspired writer of Hebrews seemed to think that this meeting together was important.

Let us consider how to stir up one another to love and good works, **not neglecting to meet together**, as is the habit of

some, but encouraging one another, and all the more as you see
the Day drawing near. (Hebrews 10:24–25, emphasis added)

The meeting together is important! We should by no means neglect it. However, I have said it before and I will say it again: You don't
have to be at church to worship God.

This truth is so important for us as worshipers. I am big on corporate worship. I cannot stress enough how important corporate worship is for us (or to God, for that matter), but corporate worship is at
its absolute best when private worship is also a regular reality. In the
case of private worship, I would use the word "regular" to mean "daily."

When I traveled overseas as a missionary, I had the experience of
being in a nation, predominantly of a different religion, during their
holy month. The adherents of this particular belief celebrate their holy
month by starving themselves throughout the day and breaking their
fast each night when the sun goes down. One of my friends who practiced this religion invited me to participate in the breaking of the fast
one night, so I went. I wasn't very hungry, because I had been eating
throughout the day, but I thought it would be a neat experience. What
I witnessed was, quite frankly, disturbing.

A dozen or more people were gathered around a banquet table,
staring at the feast before them with bulging eyes, twitchy hands, and
rumbling bellies. As soon as the sun went down and the call to break
the fast rang out through the city, fingers began flailing, and food went
flying everywhere! I kept my own hands back (mostly out of fear that
they would be mistaken for food in the midst of the madness), but
my friends devoured every last bit of food on the table. Even if I had
wanted to participate, I would have had to jockey for position. A few
minutes later, with sauces and shreds of chicken stuck to their hands
and mouths, my friends sat down and reclined deeply into their chairs,
completely stuffed.

Is this a picture of our corporate worship settings? Do we come so
starved for the things of God, so desperate to dig in for ourselves that

we become oblivious of those around us? Or are we so filled by other things (like I was) that we don't really even participate at all? Perhaps we just stand back and watch with intrigue and curiosity.

There is a better way. Jesus reminded his disciples to pray for their "daily bread." As worshipers, we should be praying for our "daily bread" and regularly meeting with God on our own. We don't have to "fast" from God and then try to stuff ourselves during corporate worship. God is with us and is available to us all of the time—every single moment of every single day. Let us regularly taste and see that the Lord is good!

Still, when we come together, we should come hungry for God to show up in ways that only happen during corporate worship. Let's not allow ourselves to be so full of other things that we are indifferent towards God. Come hungry… but not starved.

NOTES

21

GIVE A FISH
OR TEACH TO FISH

There is an old saying that goes like this: "Give a man a fish, and you feed him for a day. Teach a man to fish, and you feed him for a lifetime." This principle is worth considering when it comes to leading our people in worship.

As worship leaders, we have the distinct privilege of giving people "fish" week after week. We are the ones who are doing the hard work of preparing a set list, practicing the songs, rehearsing the songs, and then, ultimately, serving up the songs during our church worship gatherings. This is good!

There is absolutely nothing wrong with giving the people a weekly dose of fresh "fish" that is served up and ready to go, but let's not make that our only priority. Part of our job should be to teach the people to "fish" for themselves.

Dropping the fish analogy for a moment, let me communicate very clearly: I am talking here about teaching the people to praise and worship God apart from our weekly gatherings.

Many of the people that we serve week after week by leading them to the Father through musical praise and worship do not realize that He is just as accessible (sometimes even MORE accessible) outside of the assembly. Many fall into the trap of thinking that the only time they can successfully connect with God is when we are leading them in musical worship. Sadly, we tend to be the very ones who are laying that trap.

Yes, we should continue to give "fish" to our people on a regular basis. It is good and right for us to do the work and prepare a ready-made meal for our people to be a part of. But we also need to be teaching our people to "fish" for themselves, on their own, without us. Here are just a few tips that can help to that end:

Encourage daily worship, Bible reading, and prayer. While you are leading your people in weekly musical worship, take a moment to encourage them in their daily, personal walk with Christ. Saying something as simple as, "I hope your daily Bible reading and prayer this week was rich," can go a long way in communicating that you actually want them to be pursuing God on their own.

Model daily worship, Bible reading, and prayer. This can be tricky because you are not exactly inviting people into your own private prayer closet. You can, however, still make references to what the Lord has shown you throughout the week as you have faithfully spent time with Him. Sometimes I start a song with a comment like, "This week as I was spending time with God, I felt like He was really revealing this truth to me, and I wanted us to have a chance to sing it together."

Offer great resources. If there is a great article, book, daily devotional, worship album, or Christian radio station that you have found to be exceptionally helpful to you in your walk with Christ, take a moment from the stage to encourage people to check it out.

Look for ways to become less. One simple way to communicate that you want your people to connect with God without you is to be actively raising other people into your position. Look for Spirit-filled, good-hearted, potential worship leaders, and work with them. Train them. Give them opportunities to either lead a single song, or even the full worship set.

Pray for your people. Prayer is powerful. Prayer changes circumstances, and it changes hearts, including our own. If you want to see your people actively pursuing God on a daily basis without feeling like they need you to lead them, then you need to be actively praying for them, and asking God to make that a reality in their lives.

NOTES

22

Polen Band

YOU CAN TUNE A PIANO...

The American rock band REO Speedwagon released an album in the late 1970s called *You Can Tune a Piano, but You Can't Tuna Fish.* I don't know why, but that is really funny to me.

Let's get super practical and talk about one of the foundational aspects of leading worship: **tuning.**

If you are leading worship from a keyboard, you probably don't have to worry too much about this all-important part of leading worship. However, if you are leading worship—or are a part of the band—with any stringed instrument (including the piano), then you need to be in tune. Here are a couple of tips, in no particular order, to help you to that end:

Invest in a good tuner, and use it. Even if you have no other gear on stage with you, you should have a tuner! There are many different kinds available. You can use a clip-on or an in-line (stomp box, pedal, or rack mount). There are pros and cons to each type of tuner, but whatever your preference, be sure that you have one, and that you are using it.

It is a good idea to tune between songs. Many people falsely assume that once their instrument is in tune, it will stay that way for the entire set. This may be true, but I wouldn't count on it, unless, of course, you are playing a piano. I try to check tuning between every song, if the transition allows, and often even in the middle of songs, or whenever my instrument is not needed at that moment. A tuner with a mute function is key here.

The age of your strings matters. If you are playing the piano, there is not much you can do to change the tuning on a weekly basis. I would still recommend having the piano tuned professionally at a minimum of once per year. For every other stringed instrument, the age of your strings really matters. Guitar strings, especially, are susceptible to going out of tune with age. I recommend making sure that any guitar strings you use on stage are less than one month old. By that I mean the strings were put on less than one month beforehand.

Change ALL of the strings. If I am in the middle of a set and a string breaks, I will try to quickly replace it with a single string. However, in most other applications, it is best to change ALL of the strings. This is because new strings are brighter, and old strings are dull. The new string will literally be louder than the older strings and will give your instrument a poor tonal balance.

New strings need to be stretched. If you walk on stage with brand new strings that have not been stretched, you will be fighting the tuning for the entire set. When I am finished re-stringing, I always tune, stretch the strings, retune, stretch the strings again, and retune again.

Always re-tune when putting on or taking off a capo. The capo is a marvelous tool that allows you to play your preferred chord voicing in a completely different key. I love using a capo. However, no capo is perfect, regardless of what the marketing team says! Every time that

I put a capo on or take one off, I re-tune my strings to make sure they are in tune.

Intonation matters. If the intonation of an instrument has not been set properly, you will never get the instrument in tune across the board. Many times I have witnessed guitar players strum chords that are nicely in tune within the first five frets, but then they jump up to the twelfth fret and beyond for a lead part that is heinously out of tune. Even though their fingers are technically on the correct frets, they are not hitting the right notes. Intonation matters.

Pressing too hard changes the note. Even if the intonation of an instrument has been properly set, the player's touch matters immensely. If you press too hard on the correct fret, you will no longer be playing the correct note.

NOTES

I'VE PLATEAUED... NOW WHAT?

One of the most common questions that I am asked by musicians is, "How do I get better?" This question is typically coupled with a statement like, "I've plateaued..." or, "I don't know how to grow from here..."

My advice to people who ask this question is always the same. I'll admit that it is a bit counter-intuitive, but it works.

The answer comes in two parts. The first part is a question: **Whom are you teaching?**

I know. That question sounds crazy. "I am the one who wants to get better! Why are you asking me who I am teaching?"

Here is the deal; the best way to grow is to teach. Our default tendency is to want to receive instruction for ourselves (in the privacy of

our own homes through YouTube, if possible). This is strictly a con-
sumer mentality. It can, quite honestly, be indicative of a selfish mentality. The irony is that we will actually begin to grow when we begin
to invest what we have into someone who has less.

Are you surprised to hear this? You shouldn't be. It is a Biblical
principle.

> Give, and you will receive. Your gift will return to you in full—
> pressed down, shaken together to make room for more, run-
> ning over, and poured into your lap. The amount you give will
> determine the amount you get back. (Luke 6:38, NLT)

If you want to learn, start teaching!

On this note, here is an important tip to keep in mind: **You are
never too young to teach, and you are never too old to learn.** I have
found, when teaching others, that I really do have something to offer
people who are older and wiser than I am. I also have a lot to learn
from people who are younger and less experienced.

Helping someone else work through a challenge they're facing often leads me to discover other ways to do it. They may not do it my
way, but perhaps their way is better than mine. I have also discovered,
while preparing a lesson, that I really don't know what I am talking
about. That's okay! That forces me to figure something out before I
am able to present it well to others. Do you see how teaching actually
causes us to grow?

The second piece of advice that I offer to people who desire to
grow is simply this: **simplify.**

Our tendency as musicians is to want to be able to do all kinds of
things, but we end up doing all kinds of things at a mediocre skill level.
We become truly great at nothing. This typically happens because our
desire to do all things causes us to take a lot of shortcuts, and we never
truly learn how to do one thing well.

Drummers will add all kinds of fills to cover up the fact that they
can't actually keep a beat.

Guitarists will be super busy on the fretboard to cover up the fact that they don't actually know when to play.

Singers will add vibrato and inflections because they cannot actually hold a note.

If you want to get better, if you truly want to grow, try this: focus on replicating exactly what is on the record. No extra fills. No variation. Exact replication. Perfect the art of emulating what was played on the original recording note for note (no shortcuts), and you will be amazed at how other things will come easily. In the process, you will learn to make far better artistic decisions for the future, and you will truly become great at something.

NOTES

MAN LOOKS ON THE OUTWARD APPEARANCE...

There is some incredibly helpful insight hidden in plain sight in one of the Old Testament's most oft-quoted passages. The passage comes in the context of Samuel going to the house of Jesse to anoint the new King of Israel. Jesse had seven of his sons pass before Samuel, and although they all looked quite impressive, they were not the one that the Lord had chosen to be King.

> But the Lord said to Samuel, "Do not look on his appearance or on the height of his stature, because I have rejected him. For the LORD sees not as man sees: man looks on the outward appearance, but the LORD looks on the heart. (1 Samuel 16:7)

Typically, this passage is used to point out the all-important truth that God sees our heart. He looks beyond the physical reality into the spiritual and emotional reality. He knows when we are being authentic and when we are being fake.

This is critically important for us to remember as worshipers who are on stage, leading God's people into an awareness of the awesome presence of God. We may be able to fool the audience into thinking we are authentic worshipers, but we will never be able to fool God. He looks on the heart!

Tuck this truth into your back pocket and never forget it. Of course, it is important that we are real before God. Of course, He sees right through us when we are merely offering lip service even though our hearts are actually far from Him. Of course, the omniscient God knows all things. However, did you catch the other important truth within this passage?

Man looks on the outward appearance…

Man is not capable of looking at the heart. Only God truly knows the heart.

Do you know what that means? It means that, although God knows our hearts, man can only know what is happening on the inside of us when we allow it to affect the outside of us.

In other words, if we are filled with joy by the fact that God loves us, God knows that… but man can only know our joy when it expresses itself in something like an exuberant smile.

If we are overcome with a desire to submit to Jesus as our Lord, God knows that… but man can only know our desire to submit when it expresses itself in an expression such as arms raised.

When our hearts burn within us due to the excitement of knowing God is with us, and He is in control, God knows that… but man can only know our excitement when it expresses itself in actions like shouting, jumping, clapping, or dancing.

You get the picture.

As worshipers and worship leaders who have been called to lead others in authentically expressing their worship to our amazing, awesome, omniscient God, we have to remember that they cannot see what is happening in our hearts. Man looks on the outward appearance. This truth should also remind us that more may be going on in their hearts than what we are able to see.

First and foremost, yes, we need to get our hearts right before God. We will never be able to fool Him (not that we wanted to, anyway). Remember to keep that truth in your back pocket.

But when you are on stage, you are not on stage for God's sake. He sees every worshiper in perfect view, whether they are on stage or not. Therefore, when you are on stage, it is for the sake of man. They look at you. They follow your lead. They want to know what is happening in your heart, and there is really only one way for them to find out.

Man looks on the outward appearance. Let them see what is happening in your heart.

NOTES

REMOVE THE
OBSTRUCTIVE CRUTCH

Let's say that I invited you to my home. You accepted my invitation. You took the time and put forth the effort to get into your car, drive to my house, walk up to my front door, and knock. I answered... from behind the door.

In fact, let's say that I spent the duration of your visit attempting to converse with you from behind my door. Perhaps I poked my head around it just a bit, but for the vast majority of our time together, I consistently made eye contact not with you, but with the door. How would that make you feel, as an invited visitor to my home? Probably not very good.

Worshipers, worship leaders, musicians, it is time to remove the obstructive crutch! By "obstructive crutch," I am referring to the music stand.

When I was much younger, I traveled around playing music in bars. Our typical set was four hours long. One time while playing at a bar in Nashville, TN, the band scheduled to play after us never showed up. We were asked to play a second four-hour set. We played from 6:00 pm to 2:00 am with only a few fifteen-minute breaks. We NEVER used music stands. Everything was memorized.

Why would we do that? There are several reasons why we—and every other band that I knew—ditched the music stands long before we ever hit the stage.

We couldn't connect with the audience with that obstructive billboard right in front of us. How could we maintain eye contact with the audience AND with the song sheet? We couldn't! It was either connect with people or with the podium, and the people were a much higher priority. We wanted to see them and wanted them to see us. That is how ordinary people communicate.

The transition (of rustling papers) was terrible and totally killed the momentum. There is nothing worse than ending a high-energy song only to experience the thirty seconds of everyone flipping pages trying to find their place in order to start the next song. Yuck!

We realized that the stand was actually a crutch that kept us from growing stronger. Before the days of cell phones, I had phone numbers memorized. (I still have those old numbers in my head.) Then I got a cell phone, which memorized the numbers for me. Guess how many numbers I have memorized since! Probably about zero. The same is true for the music stand. YOU CAN MEMORIZE THE MUSIC! You just don't, because you don't feel like you have to. Well, I am telling you that you have to! So many of the songs that we sing in church are just scripture put to music; what is wrong with hiding God's Word in your heart and meditating on it day and night? Nothing! As long as you use the music stand and neglect the ultra-rewarding practice of memorizing the songs, you will forfeit the benefit of being able to pull out a song and lead worship any place, any time. Many a campfire has benefited from memorized worship songs!

It's not actually doing what you claim it is doing, anyway. I have seen worship leaders stand with their eyes glued to the music stand, only lifting them long enough to look at the lyrics projected on the back wall. (They apparently forgot there was an audience to connect with!) And, in spite of their supposed focus on the music, they still sang the wrong lyric or played the wrong chord!

Guess what... that music stand is not actually doing what you claim it is doing. It is not making you better. It is not making things less awkward. It is, in fact, doing the very opposite of both of those things. Until you take your eyes off of the song sheet, you will never really be able to FEEL the music, which is essential to getting better. As long as you stand with a barrier between you and the audience, it is going to be a bit awkward.

So stop. Stop using it. You can do it. If we ditched the music stands for four-hour gigs in a bar, you can do it for thirty minutes of worship in a church.

NOTES

WORSHIP MUSIC PIE

I love pie! I don't know about you, but I find pie to be super scrumptious. I am partial to blackberry, but I have a lot of favorites when it comes to pie.

When I think about music, I think about pie—not just because I love both pie AND music, but because thinking of a pie helps me to remember a fundamental musical principle.

There are many ways to slice up a pie, but each "slice" is just as good (and important) as the rest.

If I had a pie and I wanted to share it with you, I would have to slice it into at least two pieces. The nice thing to do would be to slice it into two identically sized pieces, but if it is a blackberry pie, my slice may end up being bigger than yours (hehe). If I had a pie and I wanted to keep the whole thing for myself, then you wouldn't get any.

If I had a pie and I wanted to share it with seven other people, I would have to slice it into eight pieces. Again, it would be ideal for the eight pieces to be of the same size, but that doesn't always happen. Either way, there is only one pie, and the number of slices depends on how many people will get a piece of the pie.

This is how we should think about music, as well. A good song is like a good pie. Each slice represents a different piece of the song's instrumentation.

If the instrumentation consists of just me playing the guitar and singing along, then I get the whole pie. I can strum however I want. I can sing my heart out. I get the whole pie!

If, however, we add another person (let's say a keyboard player), then it changes the way I need to slice up the pie. I can no longer play as if I get the whole thing. I need to play less on the guitar to make room for the keyboard, who is also leaving room for me. There is only one pie, and we need to slice it up so that everyone gets a piece. My piece may be a bit bigger than the keyboard player's piece, but that just means I can play a little more while they play a little less.

A common mistake that I see so many worship teams making is that the musicians and singers are all performing as if they get the whole pie. It doesn't work that way! That is not music... that is just noise.

If you have a four-piece band, let's say acoustic guitar, bass guitar, drums, and electric guitar, then each musician should play as if they represent one-fourth of the song. When you add the lead vocals and a background vocalist, each musician's slice gets a little smaller still. As you continue to add musicians and vocalists, the slices need to keep getting smaller and smaller. There is only one pie!

Admittedly, the lead vocalist and lead instrument may get a little bigger slice than the others, but each part is just as good (and important) as the rest.

Worship leader, musician, singer; think about your typical Sunday morning scenario. How many people are a part of the instrumentation? How many slices need to be carved out of the musical pie? How big should your slice be? Are you trying to do too much, taking for yourself a bigger slice than you ought? Are you doing too little and just taking a tiny slice when you really should be doing more?

If you can think about music as being like a pie and figure out how to divvy up the right-sized slices for you and your fellow worship team members, you will be well on your way to making great music. So go ahead and reward yourself with a sweet, succulent slice of blackberry pie!

NOTES

27

FOCUS TRACK

ACOUSTIC GUITAR

The acoustic guitar is the quintessential worship music instrument—perfect for stages, prayer closets, and campfires around the world! It is hard to imagine the typical worship team existing without an acoustic guitar, and rightly so. The acoustic guitar, as imperfect of an instrument as it is, continues to be the most foundational piece of nearly every worship team ensemble on the planet. If you are an acoustic guitar player or a worship leader who is trying to speak the acoustic guitar player's language and give them direction, here are some helpful tips to keep in mind (appearing in no particular order).

The **fundamental frequencies** for the acoustic guitar typically range from 82Hz to 392Hz, with the bottom E ringing at 82Hz and the third fret G on the top E string ringing at 392Hz. That fundamental frequency range covers basically every open chord note played within the first five frets. Obviously, there are harmonics in play, and adding a capo changes the range substantially, but the acoustic guitar is naturally a low to low/mid-range instrument.

Using a capo is the easiest way to play the acoustic guitar in different keys. By simply learning the G, C, D, and Em chord, you can pretty much play in every key by playing those same chords with the capo in a different position on the fretboard. That is a great trick, but it is not really the best use of a capo. The capo is most helpful in allowing you to achieve a different "voicing" for the key in which you are playing. Some songs simply sound better in the G voicing—even if you are playing in the key of C, for example. By using a capo, you will typically utilize different frequencies, which could be very helpful depending on your worship team instrumentation.

If you have a **second acoustic guitarist** in the band, consider having that guitarist use a capo and play in a different voicing. Also, to keep the music crisp and clean, have that guitarist use a different strum pattern. Perhaps they play only whole notes during the verse and add dynamics by strumming sixteenth notes in the chorus and bridge.

The **"musical buddy"** for the acoustic guitar is the **hi-hat**. If you are wondering what kind of strum pattern you should use, listen no further than the hi-hat. The acoustic guitar often gives tonal expression to the drummer's hi-hat. In fact, a great strumming technique is to use all down strums to match a quarter note rhythm on the hi-hat, and solid up-and-down strums to match an eighth note rhythm on the hi-hat.

Don't be afraid to use **all down strums** when playing acoustic guitar within the context of a band; sometimes that sounds the best. If you are on your own or playing in a small band, you may need to consider your instrument to be the main percussion piece, and you may need to strum your heart out to create an effective groove. However, when the acoustic guitar is played within the context of a full band, treating it like a percussive instrument is a sure shortcut to Sloppyville.

Good dynamics are achieved more through the strumming pattern than through strumming intensity, especially when you are playing acoustic guitar within the context of a full band. Acoustic guitar players often make the mistake of thinking they have to strum harder when the song is supposed to be really big, dynamically. In reality, the dynamics are typically already changing with the other instruments in the band, and the acoustic guitarist's role is to either remain a solid rhythmic foundation or simply add more subdivisions in their strumming. On the flip side, changing your strumming intensity is a fun way to break a lot of strings... so there's that.

Consistency is key. The acoustic guitar is such a solid, foundational worship music instrument. To play it well, you need to pick a strumming pattern that you can play well for the duration of the song. Other instruments may be coming and going as the song progresses, but the acoustic guitar will typically remain throughout. This is creating good dynamics, by the way. Sadly (for the guitarist), the acoustic guitar will often get lost in the mix as the song progresses. This is not a problem. Don't panic! In fact, many members of the congregation will typically only notice the acoustic guitar when it is played poorly. Don't do that. Play it strong. Play it well. Play it to the glory of God.

NOTES

FOCUS TRACK
BASS GUITAR

The bass guitar is the groove section of the worship team. I wouldn't go as far as to say, "It's all about that bass," but a well-played bass guitar will get the congregation grooving better than any other instrument on the stage. Of course, for that to happen, it needs to be played well. If you are a bass guitar player or a worship leader who is trying to speak the bass guitar player's language and give them direction, here are some helpful tips to keep in mind (appearing in no particular order).

The **fundamental frequencies** for the bass guitar typically range from 41Hz to 165Hz, or maybe 220Hz. The bottom E rings at 41Hz. If you are using a five-string bass, your low B rings around 31Hz. That is REALLY low. Most worship team bass players won't venture past the E note on the D string, which rings at 165Hz. Some more advanced bass players may find their way to the A note on the G string, which rings at 220Hz. With the bass guitar, there are a lot of harmonics in play, so while the fundamental frequencies are in the low range, most of the musical frequencies are actually found in the low/mid and hi/mid range. The "soul" of the bass will often be found in the 400Hz to 800Hz range, and the "pluck" or "attack" may be anywhere from 1K to 3k. A great-sounding bass will typically be found by cutting the unwanted frequencies from 40Hz to 3K, rather than by boosting the "good stuff."

The bass guitar's **"musical buddy"** is the **kick drum.** The groove of a song is often found (or created) by having the bass player pluck the notes of the chord progression identical to the pattern and rhythm of the kick drum. The bass guitar gives tonal expression to the kick drum.

Good dynamics are achieved by adding subdivisions between the kick pattern at big moments of the song. For example, if the kick drum is hitting on the first and third beat of each measure, then the bass guitarist should also be plucking the notes of the chord progression on the first and third beat of each measure. In this case, they would both be playing half notes. That works well for a verse. However, when the chorus starts, the bass guitar player can add dynamics (making the song sound bigger) by switching to quarter notes, and plucking the notes of the chord progression on every beat of the measure, even though the kick drum is still hitting on the first and third beat. When the chorus is over, the bass player can switch back to playing half notes to match the kick. This will essentially help to bring the song back down, dynamically.

While your plucking pattern may seem simple and repetitive, **it doesn't need to be played in the same position for the entire song.** A good approach to playing a song may include plucking the notes up the octave on the first and second string during the verse and then down the octave on the third and fourth string for the chorus. Play around with how you think the song can best be musically communicated, and always listen to what the other instruments are doing. The bass guitar is not a lead instrument, but it can sure make a huge difference in the overall expression of the song. When the bass guitar is solid, the song just feels right.

Bass runs can be a lot of fun and really make the song groove, but they should be used sparingly and intentionally. Bass players are notorious for getting bored (probably because they only play one note at a time, and typically only use the bottom two strings). To counteract their boredom, an amateur bass player will fall prey to running amok. This is bad. Don't do this. Admittedly, it can result in the bass player sounding really good, but the trade-off is that the band ends up sounding really bad.

Because the bass guitar is being played all over the fretboard (remember that many bass guitarists only use the bottom two strings), it is imperative that the bass guitar player **properly intonate** their instrument. This means that they set the action and string length to ensure that the open string and the same string held down at the twelfth fret produce the same note (though an octave apart from one another). If this is not the case, it needs to be fixed! If it is not, all of the hairs on the back of your neck may rise up to give you the standing ovation that you deserve.

NOTES

FOCUS TRACK
DRUMS

So much of the modern worship music sound comes from the drums. While some churches still think that "drums are of the devil," and while it is true that you do not need drums in order to worship the Lord, drums are arguably the most important instrument in worship music today. By that, I mean the drums, probably more than any other instrument, can make or break the entire worship set. Other musicians on the stage can hide their mistakes reasonably well. Not so the drummer!

Don't fear. If you are a drummer or a worship leader who is trying to speak the drummer's language and give them direction, here are some helpful tips to keep in mind (appearing in no particular order).

The **fundamental frequencies** for the drum set are all over the place; the drummer is essentially playing five to ten instruments all at once. The fundamental frequencies of the kick drum may be anywhere from 20Hz to 100Hz, while the fundamental frequencies of the cymbals may be anywhere from 8K to 20K.

The fundamental frequencies are not the only aspect of the drums that are all over the place. The **dynamic range** of an acoustic drum set can be anywhere from 70dB to 112dB, which is REALLY LOUD! Drummers need to keep this in mind as they play, as a loud drum set can drown out the entire worship team and move the whole experience from music to noise. Noise is not what we are going for! Hitting the drums lighter, playing with lighter sticks, using rute sticks, or even using an electronic drum set can be an ideal solution for drummers in a typical church setting.

The drummer's **"musical buddy"** is the **metronome**. If you can't use a metronome while playing live, ALWAYS use it to practice with. Especially use it when practicing your fills. The metronome doesn't lie; you really ARE that far off the beat when coming back from a fill! The most common phrase I hear from drummers who are just starting to play with a metronome is, "This thing is not working right!" Yes, it is.

Good dynamics are achieved by adding intensity, but also by changing up which components of the drums you are hitting, or how you are hitting them. For instance, you can be playing a closed hi-hat through the verse, and by simply opening the hi-hat in the chorus, you can make the song sound bigger. You can play on the rim of the snare during the verse and then strike the center of the snare for the chorus. Or, you can add subdivided tom hits in the chorus, along with a crash cymbal on the first beat of every measure to increase the dynamics of the song. Of course, because of the dynamic range of the drums, simply playing harder will increase the dynamics of the song.

Remember the KISS method (Keep It Simple, Stupid). Too many drummers try to do way too much. Most of that extra playing is unnecessary at best and distracting at worst. As a drummer, do not play more than the song requires, and don't attempt to play too far above your skill level. There is no faking it on the drums. You are exposed. Everyone (even non-musical people) will know when you are attempting to play a beat that you, in fact, cannot play. So do yourself a favor and keep it simple, stupid.

Avoid unnecessary, non-musical fills at ALL times. I once played with a drummer who added a fill at the end of every single measure. He did this because he was bored (and not very good). The irony is that his playing was actually boring because you began to anticipate the fact that every line would end in a fill.

Technique matters. If you want to prolong the life of your cymbals and drum heads, learn how to hit them correctly. The old joke is that playing drums is "just a matter of hitting things." No. Playing drums well consists of much more than that! One technique worth mastering is the 75/25 technique. Try playing the kick and shells at 75% volume while playing the hi-hat and cymbals at 25% volume. This basic dynamic starting point will typically give you the best balance of volume.

Consistency is key. The entire band is depending on you to play the same thing every time. Every other instrument builds off of the drums, and when the drums fail to produce a solid, dependable, consistent foundation, it will throw everything else off. So map out the song, take notes, and actually use the notes that you take.

Be smart with your arrangement. Simply playing each part of the song differently from the previous part is not enough. Think through the journey on which you want to take people when they listen to the song. Where should you be big, busy, and loud? Where should you be small, sparse, and quiet? Think through the song and play intentionally.

There is a time to be silent. Not every song needs drums, and not every part of every song needs drums. One of the most powerful techniques you can learn as a drummer is the art of playing absolutely nothing—until just the right time.

NOTES

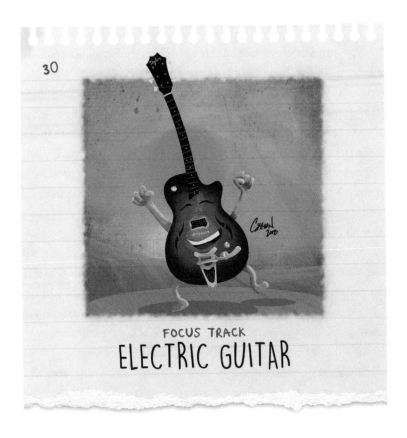

FOCUS TRACK
ELECTRIC GUITAR

The electric guitar is arguably one of the most important and distinctive instruments in establishing the classic contemporary worship music sound. However, I need to make an important (though unpopular and potentially hurtful) statement about the electric guitar from the onset: **the electric guitar should NOT be considered a foundational instrument** when it comes to church worship music.

I know, I know... it kind of hurts me even to say it, but I think this is a true, helpful, and important statement to begin with as we take a closer look at the electric guitar as it pertains to the typical church worship team. So, with that statement out of the way, if you are an electric guitar player or a worship leader who is trying to speak the guitar player's language and give them direction, here are some helpful tips to keep in mind (appearing in no particular order).

The **fundamental frequencies** for the electric guitar span the spectrum. Unlike the acoustic guitar, the electric is often played all across the fretboard, so the fundamental frequency of the note you are playing could be anything from the open sixth string ringing at 82Hz, to just over 1,000Hz (or 1kHz) if you are playing on the twentieth fret of the first string. That is a WIDE range of frequencies. Typically, and especially because the electric guitar is not a foundational instrument in church worship music, a good strategy for the electric guitarist is to first listen to what frequency range everyone else is playing in, and then fill the void.

The **dynamic range** of the electric guitar can be problematic. Because so many electric guitarists are getting their sound from stomp box pedals, or even separate channels on their amp, there can be a significant volume difference from one setting to the next. Of course, you can also use this to your advantage if you are willing to think critically through the song. If there is a part of the song where you need to be louder to cut through the mix or to add energy to the song, then you can set your stomp box to give you that boost you need and engage it at just the right time.

The electric guitarist's **"musical buddy"** is actually the **lead vocals,** along with the **keyboard** or other **auxiliary instruments**. Many of the signature riffs and instrumentals that become iconic, memorable parts of church worship music are just inversions of the melody line. In fact, playing the individual notes of the melody line during an instrumental is typically a great place to start when determining what to play for an instrumental. It is also very important for the electric guitar player to NOT play over top of the lead vocals. The electric guitar is not a foundational instrument. It is an extra piece that enhances the foundation. A good electric guitarist knows when to play and when not to play. Leaving space for the lead vocals and adding intentional riffs between vocal lines will typically yield the best results.

One thing that aspiring electric guitarists need to understand is that **the electric guitar is NOT a second acoustic guitar!** (It is not a first acoustic guitar, either...) I have seen far too many worship team members strap on an electric guitar and then proceed to play it like an acoustic guitar. It is not an acoustic guitar. You strum it differently. You often chord it differently. It sounds different. In pretty much every way, the electric guitar is NOT an acoustic guitar. The electric guitar plays a completely different role in the band. If you want to just play open note chords and strum along with the hi-hat, please play the acoustic guitar, instead.

The fact that the electric guitar is not a foundational instrument does not mean that it is an unimportant instrument! Quite the contrary! Many popular worship songs have a signature electric guitar riff or another part that immediately makes the song recognizable and invites worshipers to enter into passionate worship. For that reason, **electric guitar players should strive to learn the signature, recognizable parts to each song**, and play those parts as well and consistently as they possibly can. There are very few worship songs that are actually enhanced by an electric guitar player's improvising.

If you have a **second electric guitarist** in the band, consider having one guitarist play power chords down in the lower register of the frequency spectrum, or maybe play only during the chorus and/or other "big" parts of the song. The other guitarist can then focus on playing signature riffs and mini-chords in the upper register of the frequency spectrum.

Many electric guitar players find themselves on an endless (and fruitless) quest for perfect tone. They acquire pedal after pedal, guitar after guitar, amp after amp, and they are never satisfied with the sound they are making. What they fail to realize is that **so much of your tone comes not from the gear you use, but from the fingertips.** Tone is primarily in the fingertips. In other words, how you physically play the instrument is so much more important than the gear through which you are playing it.

It should still be noted that electric guitarists use a LOT of gear to create the sound they are looking for. Take the time to understand how to organize and use your stomp box effects properly. Typical stomp box effects that can be considered "essential" gear in which to invest include **tone-based effects** such as *compression, distortion,* and *overdrive,* and **timing-based effects** such as *delay* and *reverb.*

Because the electric guitar is being played all over the fretboard, it is essential that the electric guitar player **properly intonate** their instrument. This means that they set the action and string length to ensure that the open string and the same string held down at the twelfth fret produce the same note, though an octave apart from one another. If this is not the case, it needs to be fixed.

NOTES

31

FOCUS TRACK
KEYBOARD / PIANO

Though it is nowhere nearly as mobile as the acoustic guitar, the keyboard/piano is a timeless and versatile instrument often used when leading worship. If you are a keyboard/piano player or a worship leader who is trying to speak their language and give them direction, here are some helpful tips to keep in mind (appearing in no particular order).

The **fundamental frequencies** for a properly tuned 88-key piano range from 27.5Hz at the low A all the way to nearly 4.2kHz at the high C. That is an incredible span of frequencies! Taking into consideration that most keyboards have myriad other sounds available, there is no telling what frequencies you may venture into. This reality is one of the factors that makes the keyboard/piano so versatile. Of course, having the ability to play in so many frequencies does not necessitate that you should actually play in all of those frequencies!

The **dynamic range** of a classical acoustic piano is nearly as impressive as its frequency range. An acoustic piano can play beautifully soft one moment and thunderously loud the next. In fact, all of this can happen within the same musical phrase depending on how hard you are playing the instrument and whether or not you are utilizing its pedals. However, it should be noted that many keyboard players struggle to access this same dynamic range and feel on the electronic versions of an acoustic piano. That's probably okay because it is very rare that you would need access to such a dynamic range in a typical worship team setting.

The **"musical buddy"** for the keyboard/piano depends on how the instrument is being played. If the piano functions as a foundational rhythm instrument, then its musical buddy would tend to be the **acoustic guitar, hi-hat,** or even the **bass guitar.** If the keyboard serves more of a secondary role, then its musical buddy would be the **lead vocals** (along with the **electric guitar** or other **auxiliary instruments**). Always remember to pay attention to and play well with your musical buddy, leaving space for them to really shine. It is an ugly world when buddies fail to get along, and the keyboard/piano player has a lot of potential musical buddies.

If you are sitting down to play the keyboard/piano, you may want to **consider sitting on your left hand!** If you are standing, go ahead and lock it into your left pocket. I am kidding, of course, but not really. When you are playing keyboard or piano by yourself, adding the left hand brings a beautiful tonal balance to the instrument. Using the left hand can even provide that groovy bass rhythm that we all love. However, when playing in the context of the band, part of the trick for the keyboard/piano player is to figure out in which frequency range they should hang out. Remember that the keyboard/piano has easy access to an impressive span of frequencies; it can fit right into a full band mix, or it can quickly muddy the mix! An easy way to avoid the mud is by sitting on your left hand and playing your right hand in the octave above the acoustic guitar (typically an octave *above* Middle C, which rings through at around 260Hz).

If you are playing a keyboard, you probably have **access to more sounds** than you realize. Occasionally the worship leader may ask for a xylophone sound, strings, or organ; your keyboard probably has those sounds. Take some time on your own to play through the vast sound library at your fingertips, and take notes along the way. You never know when you may be asked to pull up a sound that only you can provide.

One of the sounds to which the keyboard player has unique access is called a **soft pad.** The soft pad is a sustained musical texture that sits nicely just under the mix and provides a pleasant atmospheric feeling to the listener. This works well during a song, but also between songs as the worship leader is speaking or leading into the next song. A soft pad may consist of only a few notes (typically the 1 and 5 note of a chord), and you definitely do not want to hold down the sustain pedal while switching chords, or both chords may jumble together.

Depending on your keyboard setup, you may be able to **layer different sounds.** This approach allows you to play, for example, an acoustic piano as the main instrument with a soft pad or strings sound layered beneath it. In this example, when you play a chord, you will hear the prominent acoustic piano chord, but you will also hear the soft pad or strings playing the same chord. There are countless ways to layer sounds, especially if you are using a keyboard with built-in faders or a computer with a midi controller. This approach may take a bit of research and practice to figure out, but the payoff is worth it.

If the sound system through which you are playing is running in stereo, **consider running a stereo output from your keyboard,** especially if you are using any stereo sound effects like *reverb* or *delay.* This will create a depth of sound that mono cannot effectively emulate. If the sound system is running in mono, use the left output from your keyboard. The left output is the standard output for mono, although some devices intentionally used the right output for mono and have been marked accordingly.

Because the keyboard has so many sounds from which to choose, you will want to **pay attention to the volume difference between sounds and make adjustments accordingly.** It is not conducive to the worship experience when a keyboard player switches from a low-volume soft pad to a raucous, high-volume B3 organ. This kind of adjustment sends sound men scurrying to find the fader while well-meaning worshipers lift their hands in fright, rather than in worship. This is really NOT the effect we are striving for.

NOTES

32

MISCELLANEOUS INSTRUMENTS

The typical worship team configuration for the vast majority of local congregations consists of an acoustic guitar (or two), a bass guitar, a drum set (acoustic, electronic, or percussion), an electric guitar (or two), and a keyboard/piano. In the last several chapters, we have focused on each of those typical instruments individually.

But what about the worship team that uses atypical configurations, or the worshiper who wants to offer their bagpipe, ukulele, or xylophone skills to the worship team? Let's talk about it!

If you are a miscellaneous instrument player or a worship leader who is trying to incorporate miscellaneous instruments into the worship team, here are some helpful tips to keep in mind (appearing in no particular order).

Miscellaneous instruments typically sound better when added to a solid musical foundation. There are not too many people who are lining up to hear a timpani solo, but the timpani sounds absolutely awesome when added to the solid musical foundation of an orchestra. Remember the musical pie illustration? Each slice represents a different piece of a song's instrumentation. Miscellaneous instruments typically sound best when they represent a small slice of the musical pie.

Pay attention to the fundamental frequency range in which the miscellaneous instrument is playing. If this instrument is playing in the same basic range as any of your typical instruments, then the players of the typical instruments may need to back off to provide more sonic space. There is only one pie. If you are adding more slices, you need to make the other slices a bit smaller.

Pay attention to tuning. Not all instruments are created equal. Sometimes adding a miscellaneous instrument or two means that you will have to play in a different key, one that is more comfortable for the miscellaneous instrument to be played in. In some cases, the other musicians may even have to tune a bit differently for all of the instruments to *sound* in tune with one another.

Once again, not all instruments are created equal. Most of the typical worship team instruments have an easy way to plug them into the sound system. Many miscellaneous instruments do not have an easy way to plug in. Therefore, **you are likely adding live mics to an already acoustically complex environment.** This should not deter you from working to find a solution, but be aware that extra open mics on stage often translate into extra feedback. A worship leader's dream can quickly become a sound man's nightmare!

It's okay to use a miscellaneous instrument for just one song. Sometimes there is one song on your set list that could really benefit from a violinist, and you happen to have a violinist in your congregation. *Voila!* That's great! Feel free to bring them on for that one song. It is less distracting to have them play for that one song than it is to make them be a part of every song—especially if the other songs do not benefit from the addition of a violin.

It's okay to use a miscellaneous instrument for every song. If it is working for you, go ahead and make the miscellaneous instrument(s) the highlight of the set list. Give your miscellaneous instrument(s) a big ol' slice of the musical pie and allow the congregation to experience something different for that particular morning. I would not encourage you to do this often, but an occasional "Blue Grass Sunday" with banjo, fiddle, mandolin, spoons, and a washtub could be a lot of fun!

Just because some famous recording artist used an accordion on their record doesn't mean that you have to. I know it is tempting to be cool and sound just like the record, but just because you have the same instrument does not mean it sounds the same as the recording. Many miscellaneous instruments have a unique sound that comes from using a technique that takes years of practice before it can be played skillfully. Personally, I would much rather hear that accordion part played on an electric guitar or keyboard instead of hearing it played poorly on an actual accordion.

At the end of the day, most worship teams use the typical setup that I described earlier because it just works. **Always remember that our job is to point people to Jesus, not distract them from Him!** Still, our God is wildly creative, and His creativity is a part of our DNA. Adding skillfully played miscellaneous instruments can be a deeply meaningful way to worship our Creator. If you can add miscellaneous instruments to your worship team, do it! If you don't have the ability, that's perfectly fine, too. Whatever is not enhancing is distracting. Don't distract people from Jesus.

NOTES

33

FOCUS TRACK
LEAD VOCALS

The acoustic guitar is the quintessential worship music instrument; the bass guitar provides the groove. The drums keep the beat, while the electric guitar provides musical distinction. The piano/keyboard is timeless and versatile, and countless miscellaneous instruments contribute to keeping things interesting. But what about the lead vocals?

There is no question that the lead vocals are the most important piece of the worship team musical pie. While the Bible repeatedly commands us to make music to the Lord, we are commanded to sing to the Lord more than twice as many times!

The singing is greater than the making of music. The lyrics are more important than the chords and the beat. Let us never forget this!

The book of Psalms is a list of "Greatest Hits" from ancient Israel. It is literally Israel's "Song Book," containing songs that the people of God used to worship Him for generations! The musical foundation for these 150 songs has long been lost, but the lyrics remain. This is important.

While it is certainly Biblical to play musical instruments skillfully unto the Lord (see Psalm 33:3), this command is only given to a specific group of people—the musicians! The music that the musicians make is for the benefit and edification of everyone, but the command to make it (and, specifically, to do it skillfully) is only for the musicians. Singing, on the other hand, is a command for literally everyone. And, quite importantly, we are never Biblically commanded to sing *skillfully.* We are simply commanded to sing.

All of this information is vital for us to consider as we look at how the lead vocals fit into a church worship team. If you are a lead vocalist or a worship leader who is trying to speak their language and give them direction, here are some helpful tips to keep in mind (appearing in no particular order).

The **fundamental frequencies** for a typical male voice range from 85 to 180Hz. The female voice ranges from 165 to 255Hz. With the lead vocals being the most important piece of the musical pie, sound men should work to carve out space in the 80 to 300Hz frequency range to ensure that the lead vocalist can be heard clearly above the musical foundation. There are many harmonic frequencies above the foundation, and the intelligibility of the vocals will be most clearly found anywhere from 300Hz to 3.5kHz, but leaving space in the foundation is a good starting point. And, since there is nothing helpful happening below 85Hz, sound men should ALWAYS use a low-cut or hi-pass filter on the vocals. This will also minimize the popping "p" sounds that can be so prevalent in the vocals.

Most wrong chords will go unnoticed by the majority of the congregation, but wrong words will be noticed by everyone. Good musicians work hard to memorize music. **Good lead vocalists should**

work hard to memorize lyrics. Personally, I like to write out the lyrics to the songs I will be leading, on paper. Doing this has proven to be an excellent approach to memorizing lyrics. Once the lyrics are memorized, I can spend more energy reflecting on the words we are singing. I can personalize them. I can own them. In this way, the songs we sing become personal prayers from my heart. That's what they were always meant to be, anyway.

Some of the best singers are terrible worship team lead vocalists. How can that be? Remember that the Biblical command is not actually to sing skillfully, but to simply sing. With this in mind, I believe that the role for the lead vocalist on a worship team is to sing in a way that invites others to sing along. When we sing on stage in a way that is overly skillful, the vast majority of the congregation cannot sing along. At this point, we are doing the people a huge disservice. Always remember that our job is to point people to Jesus, not distract them from Him! You can easily distract people from Jesus in a typical worship team setting by singing poorly, or by singing too professionally. Both approaches miss the mark.

Everyone should sing, but not everyone should sing on stage. The Biblical command to sing really is for everyone. Let everything that has breath praise the Lord! (see Psalm 150:6) I believe that the tone-deaf worshiper who passionately pours out their praise in the midst of the assembly blesses God! However, if you can't hold a note, you should not be on stage. There is no skill level requirement for the people of God to praise Him with singing. There should, however, be a skill level requirement for people to lead the congregation in singing.

Keeping in mind that the vast majority of the congregation is not overly skilled in singing (and they don't have to be!), we need to **be careful about how low or how high we sing the songs.** We have all experienced the unfortunate moment when "Happy Birthday" or "The Star Spangled Banner" was started too high or too low. How did that turn out? It usually ended with a little groaning and chins tucked deep into the chest (if the song was keyed too low), or with eyebrows raised, necks stretched out, and vocal squeaks (if the song was keyed too high). It always results in laughter, uncomfortable glances, and, ultimately, many people no longer even attempting to sing along. That is not really the effect that we are going for as a lead vocalist.

You may have an amazing vocal range, but the congregation does not. Many worship leaders I know try to keep the highest note of the melody line for congregational singing no higher than 294Hz. That note ends up being the D above middle C. I think this approach is loving and helpful. This approach may not yield the most *exciting* results (it is always more exciting to sing as high as you possibly can), but it will certainly yield the most *Biblical* results. Our goal is to invite the people to join us in the Biblical command of singing to the Lord.

NOTES

34

FOCUS TRACK
BACKING VOCALS

There is no question that the lead vocals are the most important piece of the worship team musical pie, but what about the backing vocals? How do they fit in? What is their role? Are the backing vocals just a duplication of the lead vocals, or do they have their own unique slice of the musical pie? Let's talk about it!

If you are a backing vocalist or a worship leader who is trying to figure out how to best incorporate backing vocals into the worship team, here are some helpful tips to keep in mind (appearing in no particular order).

The **fundamental frequencies** for backing vocals are exactly the same as the fundamental frequencies for lead vocals. This should be obvious, but we don't always think about it that way, which can become problematic. The fundamental frequencies for the typical male voice range from 85 to 180Hz. The female voice ranges from 165 to 255Hz. However, because the backing vocals should be considered as an instrument that is meant to enhance the lead vocals, it is generally a good idea to lower the fundamental frequencies of the backing vocals and accentuate their harmonics upwards of 1kHz (and higher).

Remember that backing vocals are not the same as multiple lead vocals. You want to tuck the backing vocals behind the lead vocals, while still letting them shine through in the upper frequencies. As with the lead vocals, sound men should always use a low-cut or hi-pass filter on the backing vocals. I tend to run the low-cut or hi-pass filter quite aggressively on backing vocals.

The dynamic aspect of the backing vocals is critical. In the typical worship team setting, the backing vocals should not be considered "choir" vocals, nor should they be considered "gang" vocals. In a choir, everyone is singing a specific part pretty much all of the time; every word and note matters. For gang vocals, we are just trying to make it sound like a bunch of people are singing. The parts don't really matter. This can be a cool effect, but you don't need to add people on the stage in order to pull off this effect—the congregation is already taking care of it.

So, how do you accomplish good dynamics as a backing vocalist? The key is to work the mic. I am a firm believer that **backing vocalists should sing ALL of the time, but they should not sing into the mic all of the time.** The role of the backing vocalist is both audible and visual. The audible side is their musical contribution. Preferably, backing vocals will enhance the music by adding harmony notes to the melody line provided by the lead vocals. (If your backing vocalists are not currently doing this, they are really just glorified gang vocalists, and they need direction and training in harmonizing!)

If your backing vocalists are singing harmony parts, as they should be, then they should not be singing into the mic all of the time. Not every line in the song needs harmony. **Great backing vocalists**

will enhance the music by working the mic as they sing. If the line does not require their harmony, they will sing along, but not into the mic. If the line requires a nice, subtle harmony part, they will sing into the mic, but not close to their mouth. If the line requires an obvious harmony part, they will sing with the mic very close to their mouth. By working the mic, they are essentially mixing themselves in and out of the song.

You may be saying to yourself, "Isn't mixing the backing vocals the sound man's job?" Well, let me put it this way: If you don't **mix yourself as a backing vocalist,** you will only ever be noticed when you are too loud. At that point, the sound man will turn you down. He will more than likely never remember to turn you back up.

The audible role of the backing vocalist is to make a positive musical contribution by adding harmony vocals at the right time at the right volume. **The visual role of the backing vocalist is to make a positive impact on the congregation**... all of the time. In normal conversation, we all prefer to talk with someone who is excited, happy to see us, inviting, and fully engaged in what is going on. The same is true for church worship teams.

Ideally, all of the worship team members will actively engage, invite, smile, and welcome the congregation into this amazing opportunity to become more aware of the presence and glory of God through the act of worship! However, most of the people on stage have other things to think about as they are doing this. The guitarists are holding their instruments in their hands and possibly preparing to push pedals with their feet. The piano/keyboard player is paying attention to the notes at their fingertips, as well as ensuring they have the correct settings engaged. The drummer is using every limb of their body to keep the beat. I'm not giving them a free pass—they should still pay attention to their interaction with the congregation. But the backing vocalists are typically standing there with no other distractions. They are in the perfect position to focus on making a positive impact on the congregation. Pray for the people. Model what a heart fully devoted to

God looks like. Clap. Dance. Jump. Smile. Worship the Lord your God with all your heart, soul, mind, and strength! People cannot see your heart, soul, or mind, but they will clearly see whether or not you are worshiping the Lord with all of your strength.

In most situations, the backing vocals remain in the background for the entire musical set. However, **there are moments, or songs, when a backing vocalist becomes the lead vocalist or even a second lead vocalist.** When this happens, it is imperative that the new roles are clearly assigned and understood. The person who was previously a lead vocalist should now assume the role of backing vocalist, applying all that was highlighted within this chapter. Similarly, the person who is now stepping into a lead vocalist role should apply all that was highlighted in the "Focus Track: Lead Vocals" chapter. The sound man, likewise, may need to adjust the EQ of each vocalist to help them better fit into their role for the moment.

NOTES

35

FOCUS TRACK
SOUND MAN

There is one vital role in the worship team, which, if performed correctly, goes completely unnoticed! That role, of course, is the role of the sound man.

Before we get too far into this conversation about the sound man, I should take a moment to point out that I will continue to refer to them throughout this book as sound "men"—even though there are plenty of amazing women who serve in this all-important role. I don't mean anything negative by it, but the reality is that we live in a world of firemen, manholes, Men At Work signs, mannequins, and sound men. (I could also talk about the fact that, as a man, I am in no way bothered by being referred to as part of "the bride of Christ," but I think we can just go ahead and move on now.)

With that quick caveat **man**ageably behind us (haha), let's move on! If you are a sound man who is trying to figure out how to best serve the worship team or a worship leader who is trying to speak their language, here are some helpful tips to keep in mind (appearing in no particular order).

The **fundamental frequencies** for each instrument are incredibly important to know and understand. That knowledge will serve you well as you aim to craft a clear and compelling mix of the instruments on stage. Go back through the "Focus Track" series and read about the fundamental frequencies of each instrument, and be sure to put that knowledge to use.

There are always **important harmonic frequencies** above the fundamental frequencies for each instrument. Some of those frequencies are pleasant, and some are harsh. Typically, the most effective way to craft your mix is by making sure that the fundamental frequencies are present, aggressively cutting the harsh frequencies, and slightly accentuating the pleasant harmonic frequencies.

Begin crafting your mix by setting a **proper gain structure.** The sound board has a LOT of volume knobs. The gain or trim knob is a volume knob. Each EQ knob is, essentially, an independent volume knob. The channel fader affects the volume, as does the master fader (obviously). There are many ways to get the volume you are looking for, but what is the best way? Just be sure to set your gain structure intelligently!

There are two basic ideas for how to set proper gain structure. One idea is to set the channel fader to unity (0dB) and adjust the gain (trim) knob on that channel until the **output** level is loud but not clipping. Since the channel fader is optimized to work from unity, this can be an effective method. Personally, I prefer a different approach. I like to adjust my gain (trim) knob until the **input** is hitting at 60 percent and then allow the channel fader to go wherever it needs to once I am actually crafting the mix. In this way, I set the gain of every channel before I even begin to craft my mix. Since the gain (trim) usually affects the monitor (or Aux Send) mix for the musicians, this method allows me to "set it and forget it" when it comes to the gain (trim) knob, and focus on the faders.

Don't overthink your job. Honestly, at the end of the day, your job is to be a glorified volume adjuster. That's it! Don't overthink it. Sure, there's a ton that can go into it, and as sound men, we should strive to continue learning about EQ and how to set compression, gates, FX, and more, but don't forget to focus on the basics! Just make sure that nothing is too loud and that the lead vocals are coming through strong, and you'll be fine.

Pay attention to the pots and pans. Still, there is much more to the sound board than just channel faders. Each gain (trim) and EQ pot is important. Each panning decision matters. On the one hand, I like to say, "Don't touch it unless you know what your adjustment is going to do and how it will affect the mix." On the other hand, you'll never learn unless you have the freedom to just mess with it. So... use a portion of each worship team practice or rehearsal to play with stuff. But don't play with anything during the service; only do what you know needs doing.

Never set the EQ for an instrument in solo mode. Probably the number one mistake that I see sound men make is to solo each channel in order to set its EQ. Don't. Just stop! That doesn't work. The solo button is for finding and fixing problems, not for generally setting EQ. If you set the EQ for each instrument perfectly in solo mode, making each instrument sound awesome on its own, I promise that you will have a terrible full mix. When it comes to mixing a band, it doesn't matter how an instrument sounds on its own, it only matters how it sounds *in the mix.* Plus, the open mics always need to be factored in.

Additive vs. subtractive EQ. Some sound men achieve their desired EQ by adding low, mid, or high frequencies to the channel. Others achieve their desired EQ by taking frequencies away. Which is better? It depends. I think you are always further ahead by subtracting offending frequencies rather than adding desired ones, but there are many ways to achieve your goal. Scientifically speaking, you do not have more of a specific frequency than what you have available to you at unity. Therefore, by adding more, you are adding something that doesn't actually exist. I would rather take away something that does exist than add something that doesn't. Artistically speaking, that additional frequency volume (that doesn't actually exist) sure does sound cool... As a side note, you will experience much less feedback by cutting, rather than boosting, EQ.

Scientific vs. artistic mixing. Mixing music is both a science and an art. The best sound men learn how to use both. I have met sound men who know the science flawlessly, but their mix sounds terrible. I have also met sound men who are super artistic, but their lack of basic EQ knowledge and application make for a harsh, hurtful mix. Learn the science and the numbers, but be sure to create something that is musical, not just mathematic.

Use the tools of your trade. For musicians, it is a metronome. For sound men, it is a decibel reader. Get one. Use it. Work with the worship leader or lead pastor to figure out the desired volume level for your space and worship service. Make sure that you stay within those parameters each service. If people complain that it is too loud or too quiet, but the decibel reader says you are right where you need to be, then simply thank them for their input while knowing in your heart of hearts that you have been a good and faithful servant.

There is so much more that could be said about the role of the sound man, but I need to at least make this one last point: **don't forget that you are working primarily with humans!** So much of the role of the sound man is technological. It can become far too easy to treat the *humans* you work with (worship leader, musicians, congregation, etc.) the same way you treat the technology. Don't do that. Smile. Care. Be a good human. Perhaps your positive attitude and personality (or lack thereof) are being noticed more than you realize.

NOTES

36

PLAY SKILLFULLY

In his book, *Outliers,* author Malcolm Gladwell makes a case (based heavily off the research of psychologist Anders Ericsson) that it takes roughly 10,000 hours of deliberate practice to truly become a "master" of something. That is a lot of hours! According to this idea, if you were to commit yourself to becoming a master of your instrument, it would only take you five years to do it... if you deliberately practiced for forty hours a week!

If you could manage to practice for twenty hours each week, it would take you ten years to become a master. Only have five hours per week to commit to deliberate practice? Well, in that case, it would take you forty years to become a master. Yowsa!

At this point, I have some good news and I have some bad news. The good news is that anyone can become a master of their instrument. The bad news is that, in all likelihood, you will probably NEVER become a master of your instrument.

I like to encourage people to practice their instrument for twenty minutes each day. I believe this is the best strategy for really getting good at your instrument. But with this twenty-minutes-per-day strategy in mind, it would take someone more than eighty-three years to become a master. At my age, I wouldn't even be halfway there, and that's if I began at birth.

The "10,000 hours" rule is fascinating research, but I have some great news for worship team members... you don't have to become *a* master in order to adequately worship *the* Master! God's rule is substantially easier than the 10,000 hours rule.

> Sing to him a new song; **play skillfully** on the strings, with loud shouts. (Psalm 33:3, emphasis added)

God's rule for worship team members is to play skillfully. That's it! But what does it actually mean? I think it means a couple of very practical things. Let's consider these ideas together.

God deserves your best, not your leftovers. Playing skillfully means putting your heart, soul, mind, and strength into it. Isn't that the kind of worship God is looking for, anyway? Put your heart into it! Don't just go through the motions. Put your soul into it! Aim to truly connect with God as you worship Him through music. Put your mind into it! Really think about what you are playing and/or singing. Put your strength into it! Set aside time to physically and adequately prepare.

Playing skillfully is all about doing your best! It is not about comparing yourself to someone else's best; it is about comparing yourself to your best. Are you giving God your best, or are you giving Him your leftovers?

It is up to the individual church leadership team to decide what skill level is required for being a part of the worship team. 1 Chronicles 25 is a chapter from the Old Testament describing how King David organized the Temple Musicians. Note that the chapter is completely *descriptive,* not *prescriptive.* In other words, that's how he did it, but it doesn't have to be how you do it. He was organizing 288 skilled musicians. Most churches don't even have 288 congregants.

Each church leadership team should decide what practical skill level is required for worship team members. Personally, I require that musicians have a basic understanding of their instrument, play well without being a distraction, and can play along with a metronome. I want them to practice on their own, know their parts prior to rehearsal, continue to grow, and, eventually, be willing to teach what they know to someone else. But that's just me. The skill level that you or your church require of worship team members may be very different. I would strongly encourage each church to think through what it means for their worship team members to play skillfully—but I don't think I would set the skill level at 10,000 hours...

NOTES

37

(GOOD) DYNAMICS, PLEASE!!

Classically trained musicians intuitively know the benefits and importance of good dynamics. Sheet music is typically written with key, tempo, and dynamics information clearly noted. Song dynamics are essential; they are one of the primary factors contributing to the emotional experience of the listener.

Sadly, unlike classically trained musicians, the typical worship team member has not been trained in proper dynamics. Most worship teams that I have observed think of dynamics in one of two main ways: either they believe everyone plays all the time, creating a sort of freight train forte, or they think lower parts are slower parts and bigger parts have the need for speed, creating a musical roller coaster for the listener.

Neither of these ideas of dynamic expression is correct, helpful, or even musical. There is a better, more effective way, and it is not difficult to grow in this area as an individual and as a worship team. Here are some suggestions that will help to that end:

Map out the song. Listen to or play through the song, and intentionally think about what each instrument should do during each section. What should happen in the intro? When should the drums come into the song, and with what kind of beat? I like to use a simple table chart that includes each section of the song (intro, verse 1, chorus 1, bridge, ending, etc.) in the top row, and each instrument (lead vocals, BGV, acoustic guitar, bass guitar, etc.) listed in the left column. As I think through each section of the song, I fill in what each instrument should do at that point (whole note strumming, sixteenth note plucking, arpeggios up the octave, low pad, quarter note kick only, nothing, etc.). See example below:

AWESOME WORSHIP SONG

	INTRO	VERSE 1	CHORUS 1
ACOUSTIC GUITAR	Finger Picking	Finger Picking	Strumming
BASS GUITAR		Whole Notes	1/4 Notes
DRUMS		1/8 Notes on Hi Hat	Classic 4/4 Beat
ELECTRIC GUITAR 1			Whole Note Power Chords
ELECTRIC GUITAR 2		Swells	Mini Chords Up the Octave
PIANO	Whole Notes	Whole Notes	Whole Notes
LEAD VOCALS		Melody	Melody
BACKGROUND VOCALS			Harmony

Include dynamics information on your chord sheet. Most worship teams do not use sheet music, which is fine, especially since most worship team members do not know how to read sheet music, anyway. The typical worship leader will give simple chord sheets to their team members. These chord sheets consist of lyrics and chords (typically the acoustic guitar chords). A slightly more thought-out version of a chord sheet will include arrangement, tempo, and song key information. Before handing out the chord sheet, consider adding pertinent dynamics information. You can easily take this information from your map of the song.

Talk through the arrangement before playing. At the beginning of your typical practice or rehearsal, take the first ten to fifteen minutes to talk through the songs. I would recommend doing this without instruments in hand. Gather everyone together and walk through the song chord sheets (hopefully with dynamics information added).

VERSE 2	CHORUS 2	BRIDGE	CHORUS 3
Strumming	Strumming	Emphasized Strumming	Strumming
Whole Notes	1/4 Notes	1/8 Notes	1/4 Notes
Hi Hat & Kick	4/4 Beat	4/4 Beat with Big Crashes	4/4 Beat
	Whole Note Power Chords	1/4 Note Power Chords	
Riffs After Each Phrase	Mini Chords Up the Octave	Mini Chords Up the Octave	Mini Chords Up the Octave
Whole Notes	Big Whole Notes	Big Half Notes	Big Whole Notes
Melody	Melody	Melody	Melody
Harmony on	Harmony	Harmony	Harmony

Make sure that everyone understands how the song should flow, when they should and shouldn't play, how you will begin and end each song, and anything else you think is relevant to communicate at this point. I think it is important to note that you don't need to communicate every single piece of information to the worship team. I would not hand out my personal song map at this point. That is simply too much information. Only communicate what you think is necessary and helpful.

Practice with a metronome. Whether it is personal practice or worship team practice, make sure you are spending ample time with a metronome. This habit helps ensure that you are not using tempo fluctuation to attempt dynamics change. When you first implement this strategy, you will probably notice yourself—or your worship team— speeding up at the big parts and slowing down for the smaller parts of the song. This typically translates to slow verses and fast choruses, with a super speedy bridge. Long builds will be especially troublesome. The more practice you can have with a metronome, the better you will be without one.

If you employ these helpful suggestions, I promise you will begin to craft more dynamic song arrangements, which will translate into more powerful times of worship.

NOTES

38

WORSHIP AS A JOURNEY

Who doesn't like a great story or an epic journey? I sure do!

One of my favorite stories is *The Lord of the Rings,* which is a journey of epic proportions! In the story, we follow our protagonist, Frodo Baggins, through various exciting episodes and many deeply meaningful moments. It is an adventure story, but also a love story. There are battles, but not on every page. There is plenty of dialogue, but also a generous amount of description. Parts of the story are lighthearted, while much of the adventure is heart-stopping. It is an amazingly well-told story, from beginning to end. The narrative draws us in, causes us to care, and leaves us with hearts full of hope.

I believe that worship leaders ought to think of worship as a journey. In reality, we have the unparalleled privilege of musically retelling the greatest story ever told. Our protagonist, God, has led His people through various exciting episodes and many deeply meaningful moments. His is a story of adventure, but also of redemption and unending love. The story we get to retell includes hard-fought battles, but not on every page. The story of God is filled with dialogue, but it also provides a generous amount of description. Parts of God's story are lighthearted, while much of it is heart-stopping. God's story is one that has been amazingly well-told from beginning to end. His story draws us in, causes us to care, and leaves us with hearts full of hope!

Of course, there is (at least) one huge difference between *The Lord of the Rings* and the story of God... the story of God is actually true! When it comes to leading God's people in worship, we should craft our Sunday set lists with this reality in mind. We are telling an incredible story, and we should aim to tell it well.

We need to remind our people of how exciting it is to follow Christ but also lead them in deeply meaningful, reflective moments. It is okay to include an upbeat, rousing song in your set list! Maybe that song is not overly deep in theology. No worries! We are leading them on an epic journey, and it is okay to just stop and celebrate along the way. It is also okay to take a moment to go deeper. Perhaps that means leading a song that helps us to consider the depths of God's love for us or even the depths of our love for Him. Maybe both. This is an important part of the journey, as well.

Don't forget that you have people in your congregation who are currently fighting their way through a vicious battle. In fact, our enemy, Satan, desires to kill us, steal from us, and destroy us every moment of every day. There is a very real spiritual war happening during every church service, whether we recognize it or not. I once heard someone say that when Satan fell from heaven, he landed on a sound board. While that is funny (and every sound man says, "Amen!"), the reality is that while we worship, we are waging war. Let's remind our people through song that God is fighting for us! He is victorious! The joy of the Lord is our strength! We are more than conquerors through

Christ! Yes, it is good to sing love songs to the Lord, but let us raise our battle cry, as well.

It is also completely appropriate to sing songs that allow us to dialogue with the Lord, or simply sing descriptive songs about who He is. I occasionally like to lead songs that are written from God's perspective. Sometimes I encourage the congregation to simply listen and receive as the worship team sings over them. At other moments, we seem to be singing more about God than to Him. This is okay, also. We are, together, reminding our souls of the myriad reasons why God alone is worthy of our praise and adoration.

Worship leaders, go ahead and mix it up a little. Provide light-hearted moments and illuminate heart-stopping truths as you lead us on this epic journey of worshiping the King of all kings. Be intentional about drawing us in, causing us to care, and leaving us with hearts full of hope.

NOTES

39

PRUNING THE MASTER SONG LIST

Worship leaders, we have to have a serious talk. This one is going to hurt, but I have to say it... it is probably way beyond time for you to prune the Master Song List.

Whether in official form or not, each church has what I call a "Master Song List." This is the list from which the church pulls songs for worship each week. When I first stepped into the role of "Music Director" at a church, they had a Master Song List of 352 songs. Yowsa! It didn't take long to realize that the list needed to go through some hard pruning.

I know; you love the songs on your Master Song List. I get it. The songs are on "the list" for a good reason. But I have to tell you that most of the songs are on the list for reasons that simply aren't good enough.

Let's do some simple math. Let's say that your church sings five songs during each service. In one full year (fifty-two weeks of five songs per week), you will lead 260 total songs. If you have 100 songs on your Master Song List, and you evenly distribute them throughout the year, that means you will play each song 2.6 times. I don't know if that means anything to you, but to me, it means that you played it in January, June, and if we round up to three, December. Since we rounded up to three, it also means that another song (which we have to round down to two) was played in March and October. That's not good.

Using a more manageable number, what if you have fifty-two songs in your Master Song List? Evenly distributed, that means you will lead each of those songs five times throughout a full year. That number sounds a whole lot better to me!

There are so many good songs out there, but as worship leaders, we really need to say "No" to good songs, and only allow great songs to make their way onto our Master Song List. Why is it important to only lead great songs? I will offer two reasons, though more could be given.

It takes a lot of collective work to play a song well. On a stewardship level, it is not loving or wise to ask your worship team to invest their precious time and energy into learning a good song that will only be used two or three times per year. It is a much better investment and will yield greater fruit if their time and energy are spent learning a great song that will be used five or six times each year.

The congregation is full of non-musicians. To musicians, it can seem like we are over-playing the songs if they show up on the set list every other month. This is not true for the typical person in the congregation. They are not listening to, practicing, and rehearsing the songs several times leading up to Sunday morning. They hear them once, and then not again for several months. This two or three times-per-year approach makes it incredibly difficult for the typical congregant to know the song, internalize it, own it, and then sing/pray the song from the depths of their soul! If we are frustrated that our people are not singing passionately to the Lord, it could be because they are still learning the song.

Personally, I like to use a Seasonal Song List approach. I get the worship team involved in selecting fifteen to twenty great slow songs, and fifteen to twenty great upbeat songs to be used for the upcoming season. Then I encourage them to invest their time into those thirty to forty songs, knowing that we will be pulling exclusively from that Seasonal Song List for the next three months. Some songs may be used five times and some songs may be used one time. If it is used only once, it is probably not a great song and doesn't deserve to be on the next Seasonal Song List. I also make sure that each song is on the Seasonal Song List no more than two seasons in a row before being taken off the list for at least one season. Doing so helps to keep the list fresh.

I also try to be intentional about introducing one new song each month. That song is introduced one week, played again for the next two weeks, gets the fourth week off, and then is played again on the fifth week. On three, off one, on one. That is the formula. If the congregation isn't singing it with fervor on that fifth week, then it was not actually a great song.

Worship leaders, please do yourself, your worship team, and your congregation a big favor... prune that Master Song List.

NOTES

40

THE PRAYER CLOSET

Scientists say that roughly 87% of an iceberg is below the water. When sailors see an iceberg above the water line, they can assume that approximately 87 percent remains unseen under the water.

In a 2009 study conducted at Virginia Tech, analysts Susan Day and Eric Wiseman discovered that the natural ratio of root radius to tree trunk was about 38 to 1. In plain terms, this means that a six-inch tree could have roots out from the trunk as far as nineteen feet. The six-inch tree that is seen is only a very small portion of the tree itself!

What is true in the natural world often leads us to a supernatural truth, as well.

As worship leaders and team members, we are on the stage, visible to the congregation, for roughly thirty minutes per week, or maybe sixty minutes if you have two services. Is this the entirety of our worship? I hope not!

Now, I understand that worship is so much more than music. Amen! But that is a different conversation. For the purpose of this conversation, I am speaking to the leaders and members of the musical worship teams. If the iceberg does not have roughly 87 percent of its actual mass underwater, it will quickly melt away and cease to exist. If the tree does not have an elaborate root system underground, it will shrivel up and die. If the worshiper does not intentionally and passionately pursue the secret times of worship, they will spiritually dry up and wither away.

I have heard far too many worship leaders and team members express that they are feeling "burned out." I don't believe in burnout. I don't think Jesus believes in burnout, either.

While Jesus was passing through a town of Samaria, he met a woman at a well. He asked her for a physical drink but then went on to talk about how he actually possessed "living water." He shared with her about how God is looking for people to worship Him in spirit and in truth. Later, his disciples returned with physical food and encouraged Jesus to eat.

> But he said to them, "I have food to eat that you do not know about." (John 4:32)

The disciples were confused. They thought Jesus was referring to physical food, and they wondered if someone had brought food to him while they were away.

> Jesus said to them, "My food is to do the will of him who sent me and to accomplish his work." (John 4:34)

Worship leader, worship team member, your food is to do the will of Him who sent you. Yes, your role is to physically be in front of the congregation, faithfully leading them to worship God in spirit and in truth. But that is only the visible part of what He has sent you to do.

Jesus found His "food" in doing the will of God. He found His strength in the lonely places to which He often withdrew in order to spend private time alone with the Father (see Luke 5:16).

Leading worship should not drain us. It should be our food. But as with the iceberg and the tree, if our public leading of worship is the fullness of the substance, the substance will not last.

Thankfully, Jesus was the example for us and gave us the secret recipe to an effective and fruitful life of ministry. I call it the prayer closet, and it is the unseen place where the vast majority of our worship should occur.

> But when you pray, go into your room and shut the door and pray to your Father who is in secret. And your Father who sees in secret will reward you. (Matthew 6:6)

NOTES

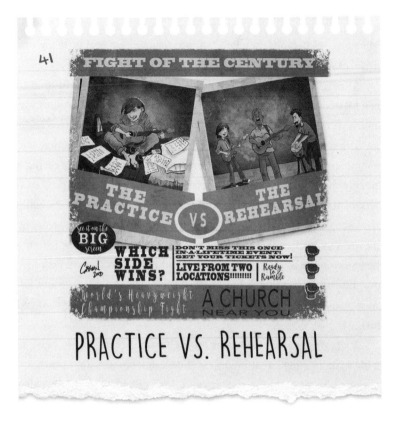

41

PRACTICE VS. REHEARSAL

In the classic 1937 film, *We Shall Dance,* Fred Astaire and Ginger Rogers introduced the world to a song written by brothers George and Ira Gershwin. The song, "Let's Call the Whole Thing Off," was performed by Fred and Ginger as they roller skated together and considered their vast differences. Among other supposed irreconcilable differences mentioned in the song, the most popular line says, "You like tomato and I like tomahto... let's call the whole thing off!"

When we approach the worship team conversation of "Practice" vs. "Rehearsal," it can feel a little like "tomato" vs. "tomahto." It's not. This conversation is not a matter of mere word choice or pronunciation. "Practice" and "Rehearsal" are two completely different things!

Most worship teams I have worked with have not spent a significant amount of time considering the difference between practice and rehearsal. By default, they will fall into focusing on and utilizing one or the other.

A worship team that wrongly focuses on "Practice" will tend to be a bit chaotic and, ironically, often unprepared for Sunday morning. Such a worship team looks something like this:

The worship team comes together for their weekly practice, and many members see the song list for the first time. Some are seeing a specific song (or two) for the first time. The entire practice time consists of team members trying to figure out most of the songs while being stopped at multiple points throughout the song to be directed by the worship leader. Direction is decided and given on the spot (though the worship leader would surely not admit to that), notes are furiously jotted down (sometimes), but most of the note-taking is fruitless because what is being practiced and decided will ultimately be changed during the service.

A worship team that focuses on "Rehearsal," on the other hand, is in for a challenging situation unless the team members have practiced on their own prior to the rehearsal. It does not work to simply call a "Practice" a "Rehearsal" and think the name change will be effective. It won't. There needs to be a function change. A worship team that correctly utilizes a "Rehearsal" looks something like this:

The worship leader gives worship team members adequate, advance notice of the entire set list and any pertinent arrangement notes (key, tempo, instrumentals, etc.). There is a clear understanding among the worship team that "Practice" is what you do on your own, and "Rehearsal" is what happens when the team comes together for their weekly gathering prior to Sunday morning. Thus, each member of the team comes to the rehearsal prepared because they have spent adequate time practicing on their own.

At the start of the rehearsal, the worship leader talks through each song, answers any questions the team members may have generated from their practice time (although these can be asked and answered in advance), and highlights key parts to make sure that each member is prepared for the rehearsal. Once the arrangements are clearly under-stood, the worship team plays through each song, stopping to address any problem areas, or even looping through problematic spots to make sure that the team is working well together. After any kinks are worked out, the team rehearses each song exactly as they practiced it. There is no need to stop the song at any point. This is a rehearsal, and the team should play the song exactly as they will play it on Sunday morning.

So which is better, "Practice" or "Rehearsal"? There is a comical line in the song "Let's Call the Whole Thing Off" in which the charac-ters played by Fred and Ginger come to an important realization. After laying out their obvious differences, they sing, "For we know we need each other, so we better call the calling off off!" The same is true in the epic battle of "Practice" vs. "Rehearsal." Both are important. Both have their place. "Practice" is what worship team members should be doing on their own (with the help of the worship leader). "Rehearsal" is what worship teams should be doing when they come together.

NOTES

42

TIPS FOR A GREAT PRACTICE

When I think about "Practice" in the context of a worship team, I think about what team members do (or should be doing) on their own time. One of the most practical ways to "love one another" is to honor one another's time. It is not loving for the electric guitarist to work out his part while the rest of the team stands around watching. The electric guitarist is practically loving and honoring their fellow worship team members by practicing their parts on their own time, prior to rehearsal, and coming to the rehearsal prepared to musically blend their part in with what the rest of the team members have also been practicing on their own.

Be a loving worship team member. Practice! I am afraid that perhaps many worship team members do not know how to effectively practice prior to rehearsal. With that in mind, here are some tried and true tips for a great practice.

Practice does not make perfect. I'm sure you have heard the old adage, "Practice makes perfect." It is a cute slogan, but it is not correct. The reality is that good practice makes better and bad practice actually makes worse. Merely playing the parts will not make you better. Practicing sloppily will train your muscles to perform sloppily. When you practice, do your best! Treat your practice as if someone were watching. The reality is that Someone IS watching. God knows and sees everything. We can honor Him and worship Him just as much with our faithful effort during practice as we can with our heartfelt performance on the stage.

Use song sheets. Personal practice is the perfect time to work out all the kinks. I like to print out the song sheets, making notes along the way as I practice the different parts. The notes will vary depending on what instrument I am playing, but they help me memorize my parts. The notes also help me to remember parts quickly if we end up playing that same song a few months down the road. Sometimes I will create my own song sheet, rather than use the one that the worship leader provided. Doing so is an especially helpful method of memorization, and I also have the correct chords on the sheet so that I don't have to continually transpose them in my mind. As soon as possible, I want to move from *depending* on the song sheets to simply having them on hand as a *reference.*

Use a metronome. Practicing with a metronome helps me get used to playing at the correct tempo. Remember that bad practice makes worse! Practicing at the wrong tempo can actually cause you to be less prepared for rehearsal. Practicing with a metronome also helps me to locate trouble spots in the song. If I find a spot where I tend to speed up or slow down, I'll be mindful of that during rehearsal, but I might also end up spending extra time practicing that particular part.

The mp3 is a liar. One common method of practice is to play along with the professional recording. While this can be helpful to a point, always be mindful that the mp3 is a liar! It will make you sound better and more prepared than you really are. At some point (sooner rather than later), you need to take off your mp3 training wheels and practice the song without the polished and perfect background of the professional recording.

Recording yourself is the ultimate truth teller. Rather than play along with the professional mp3, take a quick moment to pull out your phone and record yourself. If possible, record with a metronome clicking away, so that you can hear both. Listen back through and assess the truth of your performance. Take notes on what sounded good, and on what did not sound good. Try it again. Keep going until it sounds the way you want it to.

Twenty minutes per day keeps the unprepared nerves away. Too often our practice consists of doing nothing, doing nothing, doing nothing, and then trying to cram in a three-hour practice right before rehearsal. I get it. We're busy. But the truth is that our brains tend to shut down after approximately twenty minutes of intense concentration. Therefore, a twenty-minute practice each day is actually far more beneficial than a single three-hour practice.

Have fun. Don't forget that music is actually fun! That's probably why you started playing it to begin with. Along with that twenty-minute practice each day, throw in five to ten minutes of just playing around and discovering your instrument. Get creative. Have fun. There is a time for everything. When it is time to have fun, have fun! When it is time to really focus and practice, practice well.

A NOTE ABOUT NOTES FOR:

- **acoustic guitar:** Write down notes about strumming patterns, and when to play or not play during the song.

- **bass guitar:** Write notes about when not to play or not play, the plucking pattern for each part, and where to play fills or notes up the octave.

- **drums:** Make notes about when to play or not play, the kick and snare pattern, and whether your power hand is using an open or closed hi-hat, ride, or crash. Also, jot down notes about where specific fills belong.

- **electric guitar and keyboard:** Write notes about when to play or not play, the sound effects you are using, and where you are responsible for any signature song parts. Chart out the signature riff for quick reference.

- **backing vocals:** Underline or highlight when you should be singing directly into the mic, and plan to sing everything else away from the mic, allowing the lead vocals to be front and center.

NOTES

43

TIPS FOR A GREAT REHEARSAL

As with so many leadership realities, the effectiveness of a worship team rehearsal begins and ends with the worship leader. Yes, it is up to the individual team members to be practicing on their own and preparing themselves, leading up to the rehearsal. However, the vision for that practice time, the essential information and materials required to make that practice time effective, and the clearly communicated expectations for both practice and rehearsal all come from the worship leader. Leadership is not for the faint-hearted.

The first step to a great rehearsal is **clear and timely communication from the worship leader.** There are myriad ways to do this, but the point is not so much about *how* the information is communicated, but about *what* information is communicated, and *when*. Worship team members need to know what songs they will be playing (a set list), and the arrangement, chord progression, key, and tempo for each song (song sheets). They also need to know what day and time they are expected to be at the rehearsal, and about any other expectations the worship leader may have. Additionally, it can be helpful for the worship leader to provide reference tracks if there is a specific version of the song they are trying to emulate. This can be as simple as a Spotify or YouTube link to that version of the song, or possibly an iPhone recording of the worship leader playing a lead rhythm instrument and singing the correct arrangement at the correct tempo. Communicating a monthly or quarterly overview is quite helpful, and I would strongly encourage worship leaders to communicate with their team at the beginning of each week, as well.

As the worship leader, set clear time expectations for the rehearsal. I like to communicate to the team when I expect them to be set up and ready to begin with something like, "Please be set up and ready to make music by 7:00 pm." I will also let them know when we will be finished with the rehearsal. A ninety-minute rehearsal is perfect, so I'll let the team know they can expect to finish no later than 8:30 pm. One practical way to love one another is to respect each other's time. Worship team member, be on time and ready to play when expected. Worship leader, do not let the rehearsal go longer than communicated.

As the worship leader, communicate a clear rehearsal schedule. Let the worship team know how you intend to spend the rehearsal time. If there is going to be a break at some point, let them know in advance. Worship team members will be far more productive when they have a clear understanding of what is happening, and when. Ideally, I like to separate the musicians and the vocalists for the first forty-five minutes of rehearsal. I want the vocalists to work through the lyrics and harmony parts in a separate room, while the musicians are on the stage, working through the music. Then we spend fifteen minutes together doing a quick devotional (or a #WeeklyWorshipThought) and close that time in prayer. The final thirty minutes are spent going through the set list just as it will be performed during the service. Of course, there is no one right way to do it; this is just my preference. However you decide to do it, clearly communicate how you intend to spend your precious time together.

Check your bad attitude at the door. I know, I know, church is supposed to be a place where you can just be real with one another, right? Yes, it is, but the rehearsal is not really the time or the place for a bad attitude. Like it or not, you have a task to accomplish. A bad atti- tude is not only deflating to the people around you, but it is also highly contagious. A little leaven leavens the whole lump (see Galatians 5:9). Thankfully, a good attitude is also contagious. Be the person you would want to hang out with.

Start with a song that you all know really well. You want to start the rehearsal on the right foot! Don't spend the first thirty min- utes hammering through a song you barely know. Start each rehearsal with a song you all know well; there should be at least one of those on the set list. Start the rehearsal with some positive momentum! By starting with a familiar song, you can focus more on your monitor settings. Stop after that first song to resolve any monitor issues, then begin to work through the rest of the songs, which will likely require more attention.

Use a metronome. If your worship team uses in-ear monitors, then you should be running a metronome during the rehearsal and the service. However, even if you use floor wedges, you should use a met- ronome during rehearsal. There is simply no better tool for helping musicians learn how to play well together.

Schedule an extra sound man. Having only one sound man—or a sound man who didn't show up—has sidetracked many should-have- been-productive rehearsals! One super-practical fix is to schedule an extra sound man. I prefer to have one sound man and one stage hand at each rehearsal. With this model, the sound man can stay in the sound booth, while the stage hand runs back and forth from the sound booth to the stage to physically fix any issues that may arise—and we all know what kinds of issues can and will arise! With the sound man firmly established in the sound booth, the rehearsal can move forward even while the stage hand is troubleshooting a problem with the keyboard not being plugged in to the correct channel.

Encourage one another. Far too many of our comments during a typical rehearsal are focused on what went wrong. We want to fix these trouble spots, of course, but don't forget to highlight what went right, also. Encourage one another! Give a high five! Allow yourselves to actually enjoy being together. Each member of the worship team brings their own unique personality and skillful musicianship to the group. Together you are worshiping the Lord through music—which He created, by the way! It's a pretty awesome gig!

End with an optional jam session. Even though rehearsal has a definite ending time, that doesn't mean you have to be finished. Collectively, the typical church worship team has a LOT of creative energy. While this reality may not be overly conducive to an effective rehearsal, it can be positively channeled elsewhere. Once rehearsal is over (at the predetermined and clearly communicated time), thank everyone for their investment of time and energy... but since everyone is there, and all of the equipment is set up... you may as well have a jam session! Invite anyone—who is willing and able—to stay and play through a few songs just for fun. This can be a great opportunity to build camaraderie and chemistry as a worship team and just let those creative juices flow. Plus, this approach gives you ample opportunity during rehearsal to unleash epic, one-line zingers like, "Hey Jimi Hendrix, why don't you save that solo for the jam session...!"

NOTES

44

GOLDEN NUGGET #1

WORSHIP IS GOD'S IDEA

There is so much that could be said about leading a congregation in worship. I have been to myriad seminars and read countless articles, blogs, and books about it. There seems to be no end to the amount of information available on the subject. So with that mountain of information available to you, how can you effectively dig through it all to find what is really important?

I think there are five truths that are the most important pieces of information on the subject. I call these five truths the "Golden Nuggets of Worship Leading." You don't have to know everything. If you can just discover and focus on these five Golden Nuggets, you'll be fine!

The first Golden Nugget of Worship Leading is this: **Worship is God's idea.**

God is the one who thought up worship! It is worth pointing out that you do not have to use music to worship God, and that worship is much bigger than music, but for the purpose of these chapters, I am referring to musical, congregational worship, which God invented.

Worship is not rocket science! We have an unhealthy tendency of over-thinking worship or attempting to come up with fresh ways of worshiping the Lord, but we do not have to invent new ways of doing it. Worship is God's idea, and He has already given us a fairly exhaustive list of ways that He would like for it to be done.

For example:

Clapping hands (Psalm 47:1). While we tend to think of clapping hands as a beat-keeping percussion instrument, or as a way of applauding after a song (both of these are great, by the way), the Biblical understanding of clapping hands is actually more about agreeing with what is being presented. When we clap our hands, we are essentially saying, "Amen!" or "Let it be so!"

Raising hands (Psalm 134:2). There are many reasons to raise our hands to the Lord in worship. I like to think of asking my Daddy to hold me, or of surrendering to the Lord, or of receiving His blessing, or of engaging in spiritual warfare like Moses did while Joshua fought the Amalekites. Either way, God thought of worship, and He has clearly instructed us to raise our holy hands in worship.

Dancing (Psalm 149:3). While dancing is often considered too "worldly" for most congregations, it is actually an incredibly Biblical form of worship. In fact, King David danced so passionately in worship during the return of the Ark of the Covenant that he accidentally revealed his undergarments and embarrassed his wife.

Shouting (Psalm 47:1). God did not intend for worship to be boring or void of emotions. Perhaps the spectators' response at a championship football game looks more like Biblical worship than what we see during most church services. It is Biblical, right, and good to shout for joy to the Lord in the midst of the congregation.

This is just a small taste of what God has in mind for Biblical wor-

WORSHIP IS GOD'S IDEA

ship. The list could easily include **singing** (Psalm 96:1-2), **declaring God's works** (Psalm 105:2), **bowing down** (Psalm 95:6), **being silent** (Psalm 46:10), and more.

The point is simply that worship is God's idea. We don't have to invent new ways of doing it. He has already said much on the subject. We would do well to go straight to the source and give Him the praise that He is due in the ways that He has described.

NOTES

45

GOLDEN NUGGET #2
REMEMBER YOUR PRIMARY PURPOSE

Worship is God's idea! I think we sometimes forget that. We have an unhealthy tendency of making worship more about us than about God. We are constantly tempted to make worship more about our preferences, our thoughts, and our feelings than it is about God's preferences, thoughts, and feelings. We have to resist that temptation at every step. Worship is God's idea. He has a LOT to say about the subject, and we would do well to obey the instruction He has given.

The fact that worship is God's idea is the first Golden Nugget of Worship Leading, and it is the cornerstone for the second: **Remember Your Primary Purpose.**

This one is likely going to hurt, but it needs to be said. Leading worship is NOT your primary purpose. It's not. Yes, worship is God's idea.

Yes, it is a high calling. Yes, it is important. No, it is not your primary purpose. Your primary purpose is to make disciples.

After creating the world, being born of a virgin, living a sinless life, dying on the cross for our sins, and rising from the grave, Jesus clearly revealed the primary purpose for anyone who would claim to follow Him:

> All authority in heaven and on earth has been given to me. Go therefore and make disciples of all nations, baptizing them in the name of the Father and of the Son and of the Holy Spirit, teaching them to observe all that I have commanded you. (Matthew 28:18-20)

This is the only time throughout the gospels that Jesus uses the phrase, "All authority in heaven and on earth has been given to me." Why would He use that phrase here? I believe He is helping us see the magnitude of His next statement. The Great Commission is NOT the Great Suggestion! The boss of heaven and earth has given His followers a non-negotiable assignment. Our primary purpose is not to make music; it is to make disciples!

Does this mean that leading worship is unimportant? No! Leading a congregation in musical worship is awesome! It is a God-ordained calling. In fact, it is the one thing that God said we should do skillfully (Psalm 33:3). Leading worship is not unimportant, but it is secondary. Our primary purpose is to make disciples.

Practically speaking, you can devote your entire life to leading congregational worship and be incredibly gifted to do so. You can lead thousands upon thousands of worshipers into an awareness of the presence and glory of God by skillfully using your musical gifts, but if you fail to make disciples along the way, then you fail at what matters most.

Imagine a father telling his child to clean their room while he runs to town. Upon his return, the father notices that his child did not finish the clearly communicated task. Of course, the father would ask his child, "Why didn't you do what I told you to do?" Now imagine the child responding by saying, "Well, I may not have cleaned my room like you asked me to, Dad, but I did sing a lot of songs about you while you were gone! In fact, I even wrote a few of my own! Also, my siblings came by, so I led them in singing the songs, as well. We've been singing about you the whole time you were gone!"

I am a father, myself. I can honestly say that I would not be impressed by this response. Neither will God the Father be impressed by our disregard of making the Great Commission our first priority and recognizing it as our primary purpose! Worship is God's idea, but He is not impressed when we attempt to worship INSTEAD of obey. Obedience is God's love language. He desires for us to worship AND obey! The two are not mutually exclusive! The truth is that, by being intentional, you can fulfill your primary purpose of making disciples while engaged in any secondary purpose, including leading worship. In fact, this is what true worship is really all about.

NOTES

46

GOLDEN NUGGET #3
THREE KEYS FOR WORSHIP MUSICIANS

Worship is God's idea, and it is good! Still, our primary purpose as worship leaders and worshipers is not to make music, but to make disciples. These are two really important truths to keep in mind!

The third Golden Nugget of Worship Leading actually comes in three parts. I call this third Golden Nugget, **Three Keys for Worship Musicians.** By keeping these three keys in mind as individual members of a collective worship team, you will make beautiful music together that glorifies God and edifies His people.

1.) The BEST Musicians have the BIGGEST ears. It should probably be said that I am not referring to the literal, physical size of the ears. I am talking about the musician's ability to listen well. The best musicians have the biggest ears. A great musician will not want to hear more of *themselves* in the monitor mix; they will want to hear more of *others*. They have already put in the necessary amount of practice. They already know what they are playing and how it sounds. They don't need to hear more of themselves; they need to hear more of everyone else. By listening to what everyone else is contributing to the song, great musicians know how to fit in by playing just the right part—the missing part.

2.) There is ALWAYS a lead instrument, and it is NOT always you. Each song has a lead instrument. For some songs, it is the electric guitar; for others, it's the piano. For many songs, the lead instrument is the acoustic guitar, while some songs actually utilize the drums as the lead instrument. Either way, there is always a lead instrument, but it is not always yours. Songs very rarely have more than one lead instrument, yet the typical worship team seems to operate as if every instrument is the lead instrument. Brothers, this should not be! If there is a question as to which instrument is leading the song, the worship leader should quickly settle the dispute. If yours is the lead instrument for a particular song, then lead on, fearless leader! If yours is not the lead instrument, humbly accept your role as a rhythm or background instrument. Play that background part as well as you can, to the glory of God! When several different musicians are jockeying for position as lead instrument, the whole worship team suffers, as does the congregation.

3.) Leading a church in worship is all about SERVING. Too many musicians join the worship team because of what they can get out of it, rather than because of what they can give through it. In reality, being a part of a worship team that is leading a church in weekly worship services is all about serving.

- *We serve the song*—by playing what is needed rather than what is fun.
- *We serve the worship leader*—by helping to bring their vision for the song to life.
- *We serve the congregation*—by providing an engaging musical backdrop for them to offer their own unique expression of heartfelt praise and prayer to God.

- *We serve the senior pastor*—by setting the stage for the con-gregation to clearly hear the Word of God faithfully pro-claimed through the preaching.
- *We do not serve ourselves.* Our sinful nature will always fight to do what we want, when we want, how we want. We have to resist that temptation at every turn! Our role as a worship team member is like that of a really good chef. We skillfully prepare the food, and then we serve it to everyone else. Once everyone else has been fed, then—and only then—do we also get to enjoy the well-crafted meal. Of course, the real joy is not in eating the well-crafted meal. The real joy is in seeing others delight in what God has given you the ability to create.

NOTES

47

EQUIPPING PEOPLE IS GREATER THAN BUYING EQUIPMENT

Imagine that I nominated you to be team captain for a neighborhood pick-up basketball game. As you are choosing your teammates, you notice one potential player standing on the sidelines with the latest, greatest gear. He has the name brand headband, wristbands, jersey, and shorts. He is laced up in this year's NBA All-Star's signature shoes. He is dribbling an authentic NBA basketball. You also notice a second potential player standing next to the first. This person looks to be wearing hand-me-down clothes that are a couple of sizes too big. His shoes are decent, but showing wear. He has no ball. He just came to play. As the designated team captain, which player would you choose for your team?

The correct answer should be: "I don't know." How could you possibly know? The reality is that you simply do not have enough information to make a wise decision. Yes, we can look at the situation at face value, and we can assume that the guy with the better gear is a better baller, but the quality of the gear does not actually determine the quality of the player, does it?

This leads us to our fourth Golden Nugget of Worship Leading: **Equipping People is Greater Than Buying Equipment.**

I have worked with far too many churches that think the answer to their worship team woes is simply to invest more money. Ironically, these churches will not hesitate to invest tens (or hundreds) of thousands of dollars into the latest, greatest sound system, but they will not build hundreds of dollars worth of lessons and training into their annual budget. These churches struggle to understand that equipping people is greater than buying equipment.

In reality, a truly great guitar player can make a cheap guitar sound amazing! At the same time, an unskilled guitar player can make an incredible guitar sound really bad!

I will be the first to admit that, all things considered, good equipment will always sound better than bad equipment. (Good equipment also tends to cost a lot more than bad equipment.) Still, high-quality equipment will only ever be optimized by skillful people. Better equipment may come, in time, but it is always better to focus on simply becoming a better player.

One who is faithful in a very little is also faithful in much. (Luke 16:10)

Don't make the mistake of falling into the negative (and often wrong) way of thinking that says you would sound better if you just had better equipment. That may be true, but the bigger question is: Are you being faithful with what you have? Are you investing wisely? I'm not just talking about financial investments, but also time investments. When we short-circuit the growth process by just buying better equipment, we fail to grow and maximize our current skill level, and we fail to optimize the better, more expensive equipment that is meant for someone way above our current skill level.

Do you remember the parable of the talents, or of the minas? Invest well what you have been given, and God will cause the growth. He will provide what we need when we need it.

There is another way that far too many churches solve their worship team woes, and it needs to be addressed. When an NBA team wants to be competitive and beat the other teams in the league, they go out and hire the best players available. They don't really care from whom they take the players. They need the player, so they offer them more money than the other team was offering. I don't like this in the NBA, but I hate it in the church. Rather than going out and competing for the latest, greatest worship leaders and musicians, what if we did what Jesus did and raised people up from within? How do we do that? We do it by equipping people better—not by simply buying better equipment!

NOTES

48

GOLDEN NUGGET #5
PRIVATE BEFORE PUBLIC

Worship is God's idea! As important as worship is, your primary purpose is to make disciples, not music. The best musicians have the biggest ears, there is always a lead instrument (it is not always you), leading a church in worship is all about serving, and equipping people is greater than buying equipment. We have uncovered a lot of Golden Nuggets in the last several chapters, and I trust that they have been helpful. This final Golden Nugget of Worship Leading may be last, but it is certainly not least: **Private Before Public.**

It can be far too easy for worship leaders and musicians to fall into the false way of thinking that our public worship is what really matters. It's not. Our public worship should be the result of our private worship throughout the week. In fact, though there are exceptions to this rule, I would encourage you to **never do publicly what you have**

not first done privately. Whether that means you do not lead a song publicly that you have not first offered to God privately, or whether you should not say or pray something publicly that you have not first said or prayed to God privately, the principle remains. Never do publicly what you have not first done privately.

I once heard a prominent speaker and pastor say, "Delivering a sermon is not worship... not really. My prayerful preparation and diligent study for the sermon is the true worship." Clearly, this speaker was using hyperbolic language to make an important point. We typically think of delivering the sermon (or the song) as the true worship, but in reality, offering ourselves to God through prayerful preparation and diligent study (when no one but God is watching) is our truest offering of praise.

Practically speaking, how do we live out this principle of "private before public"? Here are some tips (appearing in no particular order).

Pray the songs to God in private. These songs are, more than anything else, just prayers set to music. One of the most powerful ways to connect our hearts to God through the songs we sing is by praying the lyrics to Him in private. Before we lead the congregation into musically praying the song together, we should first pray it out loud to God on our own. As a side note; if the song doesn't feel right to pray to God in private, then it is not a worthy song to lead in congregational worship.

Journal the lyrics of the songs to God. I like to write out the words of the songs that I will lead. This exercise helps me to further connect my heart and mind to God through the words I will be singing to Him. As I write the words, I may add some of my own thoughts in response to what I am thinking or feeling. Throughout this process, I begin to own the words of the song, even if it is a song that was written by someone else. Their prayer truly becomes my prayer. All the while, I am praying that this prayer will also become the heartfelt prayer of the congregation.

Lead worship in the empty auditorium. God has always been partial to desolate spaces. There is something special about passionately worshiping God in the same empty space that will later be filled with church members. On a solitary Saturday morning, plug it in, crank it up, and pour your heart out to an empty room that is filled with the presence of God.

Prayerfully determine what you will say between songs, and rehearse it. The personality of so many worship leaders I have met throughout the years lends itself to more of a "let's just wing it" mentality. Honestly, that approach works. But it works because it is built on the winning personality of the worship leader. There is a better foundation. What if we built our approach on the Person of Christ? What if we spent time in preparation, asking the Lord what He would have us say to the people? Yes, the Holy Spirit can give us words to say in the moment, but He can just as easily (and far more frequently) give us words in advance... if we ask Him. As an act of worship, prayerfully determine what you will say between songs. Rehearse it. Test it. Is it true? Is it edifying? Is it clear? If so, then it is worthy of saying during congregational worship. If not, go back to the Lord in prayer... thankful that you didn't blurt that silly thing out for the whole congregation to hear.

Pray for the people. One of the greatest joys of being a worship leader is having the privilege of praying for the people we serve. But that should not only happen in public. In fact, some of the deepest, most heartfelt prayers happen in the preparation. Pray for the people as they come to mind in your prayer closet. Pray for the people as you pray through the lyrics and as specific circumstances come to mind. Pray for the people in the empty room. You know who sits where. Lay your hands on the seats and pray for the people who will be sitting there. Pray, pray, pray. Do not allow your public prayers to be your primary prayers.

NOTES

WHAT ABOUT CHRISTMAS?

'Twas the month before Christmas,
When all through the church,
The worship leader was stirring,
Wondering if they really wanted to go through with all of the extra preparation and headaches of trying to facilitate a month's worth of Christmas songs leading up to the biggest celebratory service of the year...

Okay, so that's not a very good poem, but it is a fairly accurate one. As worship leaders in the twenty-first century, what do we do about Christmas?

This is not an easy question to answer, and ultimately, each church will have to come to their own conclusions. To Christmas, or not to

Christmas—that is the question! I can only offer my best advice and best practices as you determine what is best for you in your setting.

Have a plan. For too many worship leaders, Christmas somehow seems to just appear out of nowhere. One day it's Thanksgiving and the next day you are attempting to perform Handel's *Messiah*. It doesn't have to be that way! Christmas is the most wonderful time of the year. Plan ahead so you can enjoy it. Personally, I like to mix a few Christmas songs in for the first service after Thanksgiving, then sing all Christmas songs throughout the month of December. But that's just me. And that takes a lot of preparation. Maybe you prefer to mix in Christmas songs throughout the month of December or wait until the week before December 25 to do Christmas songs. Either way, just have a plan and execute it.

Recycle, Reuse, Renew. Don't feel as though you have to come up with completely new Christmas songs every year. It's been eleven months since the congregation has sung Christmas songs; last year's set list is probably just as relevant this year. Recycle old Christmas hymns, reuse the songs that went over well the year before, and feel free to renew a song or two with some well-thought-out changes.

Only make changes that improve the songs. If you are going to make changes to a song that everybody knows and loves, be warned that your changes had better be worth it! Please do not change a classic, well-loved Christmas melody "just because." That is neither loving nor wise. Baby Jesus grew up and said you would be blessed if you are persecuted because of righteousness. That verse does not apply here. Trust me, you will NOT be blessed if you are persecuted for messing up a Christmas song.

Honor your elders. The older members of your church have been singing certain Christmas songs in a certain way for fifty, sixty, seventy, or even eighty years. That is worthy of honor! Keep those members in mind as you work through Christmas song arrangements. That old arrangement that is so boring you can hardly stand it may have more meaning, depth, and sentimental value to the elderly in your congregation than you can even fathom. Don't mess with their precious Christmas memories that are older than you are. Honor your elders.

Don't feel as though you need all of the instrumentation. Some of the great Christmas carols are hard to accompany. So don't. Just put the instruments down, pick up a candle instead, and sing your heart out in honor of the King of kings who humbled Himself by being born of a virgin as a helpless, human boy. If He was willing to lay down the riches of heaven, you can lay down your instrument.

Have fun! Christmas should be a time of good news and great joy! Don't let the stress of the Christmas Set List steal your joy. Wear an ugly sweater, throw on a Santa hat, have a worship team Christmas party, wear a jingle bell wristband, and celebrate the glorious birth of our Savior through joyful music and song!

NOTES

EXTRAVAGANT WORSHIP

When I think about Biblical worship, two stories come to mind. One account is from the Old Testament, and the other is from the New Testament. Both stories, I think, powerfully illustrate what it looks like to love the Lord our God with all our heart, soul, mind, and strength. Both stories are examples of extravagant worship—the kind of worship that God rightly deserves.

In 2 Samuel 6, King David is victoriously bringing the ark of the Lord back to Jerusalem. There are a lot of details surrounding this story, but it is his attitude of extravagant worship on which I want to focus.

> And David danced before the Lord with all his might. And David was wearing a linen ephod. So David and all the house of

Israel brought up the ark of the Lord with shouting and with
the sound of the horn. (2 Samuel 6:14–15)

I love this public display of affection towards the Lord that the
king (of all people) is displaying. The king is leading the way in worship! Many of the people are following David's lead. While he is dancing before the Lord with all his might, the house of Israel is joining
along with shouting and with the sound of the horn.

Of course, not everyone felt compelled to join in. David's wife Michal was less than impressed by the way the king had acted. There will
always be those who are more than willing to point out the "foolish-
ness" of you giving yourself fully to the Lord. Perhaps they are envious
of your freedom in worship, or maybe they do not truly love the Lord
themselves. Either way, you can pray for them, and we certainly do not
want to offend people intentionally, but extravagant worship is ultimately between you and God, not between you and your critics.

In Luke 7, we see another powerful example of extravagant worship. This time it is not from a king.

And behold, a woman of the city, who was a sinner, when she
learned that [Jesus] was reclining at table in the Pharisee's
house, brought an alabaster flask of ointment, and standing
behind him at his feet, weeping, she began to wet his feet with
her tears and wiped them with the hair of her head and kissed
his feet and anointed them with the ointment. (Luke 7:37–38)

This sinful woman was willing to risk ridicule and scorn simply by
entering the religious leader's house. She freely gave an expensive gift,
humbly anointing the Lord's feet with the ointment mixed with her
own tears. She gave everything that she had, even wiping his feet with
the hair of her head.

This act did not go unnoticed by the Pharisee. He saw it and
promptly misunderstood.

Now when the Pharisee who had invited [Jesus] saw this, he
said to himself, "If this man were a prophet, he would have

known who and what sort of woman this is who is touching him, for she is a sinner." (Luke 7:39)

Like Michal with King David, the Pharisee completely missed it. In fact, he seems to be appalled by what he is seeing.

Noticing that the Pharisee was not impressed by the sinful woman's act of extravagant worship, Jesus told a simple story reminding him (and us) that he who has been forgiven little, loves little.

> And Jesus answering said to him, "Simon, I have something to say to you." And he answered, "Say it, Teacher." "A certain moneylender had two debtors. One owed five hundred denarii, and the other fifty. When they could not pay, he canceled the debt of both. Now which of them will love him more?" Simon answered, "The one, I suppose, for whom he canceled the larger debt." And he said to him, "You have judged rightly." Then turning toward the woman he said to Simon, "Do you see this woman? I entered your house; you gave me no water for my feet, but she has wet my feet with her tears and wiped them with her hair. You gave me no kiss, but from the time I came in she has not ceased to kiss my feet. You did not anoint my head with oil, but she has anointed my feet with ointment. Therefore I tell you, her sins, which are many, are forgiven— for she loved much. But he who is forgiven little, loves little." And he said to her, "Your sins are forgiven." (Luke 7:40–48)

Some of Jesus' own disciples had a similar reaction to a similar situation. (see Matthew 26:6–13)

Not everyone will understand or appreciate our bold, liberated, humble, extravagant acts of worship, but that's okay. We don't do it for them, anyway. We do it for God, who loves us, and who gave Himself completely for us.

Friends, we have been forgiven MUCH! Let us love much! Let us extravagantly worship God with all of our heart, soul, mind, and strength!

NOTES

51

MAKE A BEELINE TO THE CROSS

There was a powerful, prolific preacher who lived during the 1800s in London, England. By the age of twenty-two, he was one of the most well-known preachers in the world; many know him as the "Prince of Preachers." His name was Charles Spurgeon. During his life, he faithfully proclaimed the word of God and watched as his church in London grew to over 10,000 in attendance. With nearly 3,600 sermons given, Charles Spurgeon is still one of the most frequently quoted preachers today.

Unfortunately, with popularity comes controversy. Spurgeon is also one of the most misquoted preachers today.

My favorite Spurgeon misquote goes something like this: At one point someone approached Spurgeon and accused him of only ever preaching one message. "All you ever do is preach about the cross," they said. Spurgeon replied, "That's right. That's right. Wherever in the Bible I take my text, I make a beeline to the cross and start preaching about the Lord Jesus."

I love that story! It's not true—or at least it cannot be verified historically—but I still love it.

As worship leaders, I think this is the attitude with which we should approach leading a congregation in worship. We need to make a beeline to the cross and start preaching (musically) about the Lord Jesus!

Several generations ago, when someone wanted to know about a particular church in the area, they would ask questions like, "What is the preaching like?" Today, a much more common question would be, "What is the music like?"

The reality we have to deal with is that many people are tuning in to the music and tuning out of the sermon. I know that sounds brutal, and I do not like that reality, but it's true. Many people who come to church week after week get more of their theology from the songs we sing than from the sermons they hear.

This is not a new phenomenon; it is an old truth that has recently resurfaced. Several hundred years ago, the prominent preachers of the day recognized this reality, and they used it to their advantage. Preachers like John and Charles Wesley, John Newton, Isaac Watts (and many, many others) realized in the late 1600s and the 1700s that their people were more likely to remember songs than sermons, so they set their sermons to music. Many of the classic hymns we know and love from that time period were written by pastors. And it worked! Today, you're likely unfamiliar with a single sermon that John Newton delivered to his congregation in Olney in Buckinghamshire, England, in the late 1700s... but I'll bet you can easily recite his song, "Amazing Grace."

The reality is that we have a unique and important opportunity to fill the hearts, minds, and mouths of our fellow worshipers with deep theological truths about God. The songs we select for congregational worship are crucial, because they may be the only dose of theology that will be remembered by the typical congregant from a typical Sunday morning.

Because this is true (and significant), I plead with you; please do not spend all of that precious time singing fluffy, surface-level half-truths about God. Don't sing incoherent, merely poetic, spiritualized ramblings that make you FEEL good but lack true substance. Sing about truth that truly IS good!

Make a beeline to the cross and start (musically) preaching about the Lord Jesus! Lead your people in Biblical truth set to music. Make sure that the songs you sing clearly present the gospel, then step back and watch as the Spirit of God transforms the lives right in front of you.

NOTES

52

KEEP GOING STRONG

I want to tell you something, and it is really important. Pay close attention. Are you ready? Here it goes: **You matter.**

It's true! You matter! What you do matters! Whether you are a worship leader, a worship team member, a part of the tech crew, or whatever... what you do matters in the kingdom of God! It matters to others (whether they tell you or not), and it matters to God.

Not only what you do, but also how you do it... it matters! God cares about things like that, and He has created you to be able to do what you do well. What a good God!

When we come to the end of our days here on earth, we will want to hear the words, "Well done, good and faithful servant. You have been faithful over a little; I will set you over much. Enter into the joy of your master" (see Matthew 25:21).

The hard truth is that our role in leading worship is a lot like a narrow road with a deep ditch on both sides. On one hand, leading people into an awareness of the presence and glory of God can be a thankless job. There are so many critics and so many impossible expectations laid upon us that we can easily drift off into the ditch of despair. Don't do that! You really do matter, and what you do really does matter. Even if you never get thanked, your work and your faithfulness have been seen and will be remembered by God Himself!

On the other hand, leading people into the awareness of the presence and glory of God can sometimes be an over-esteemed role. Some people will make a bigger deal out of you than they should, not realizing that it is the Spirit of God working powerfully through you who actually deserves the praise. It can be tempting to believe the wonderful things that some people will say about you. In this way, we can easily drift off on the other side of the narrow road into the pit of pride. Don't do that. Take every compliment as an opportunity to point people directly to God.

Leading a congregation into the awareness of the presence and glory of God is a high calling.... and God has called you to do it! Awesome! Do it to the absolute best of your ability!

> Whatever you do, do all to the glory of God.
> (1 Corinthians 10:31)

There will be times when you feel as though you don't have what it takes. There will be times when it doesn't feel as though you are making a difference. There will be times when you just want to quit. Don't quit! Press in to God and trust that He who called you to it will also see you through it!

> Since we are surrounded by so great a cloud of witnesses, let
> us also lay aside every weight, and sin which clings so closely,
> and let us run with endurance the race that is set before us,
> looking to Jesus, the founder and perfecter of our faith, who

for the joy that was set before him endured the cross, despising the shame, and is seated at the right hand of the throne of God. (Hebrews 12:1-2)

There may be times when you feel like you've got it all figured out. There may be seasons where everything just seems to be going your way. Awesome! Praise God! But remember that it is not you who is doing the work, but it is the Spirit who is working so powerfully within you. (see Colossians 1:29 and Philippians 2:13) Do not allow your heart to grow full of the insidious poison of pride.

Clothe yourselves, all of you, with humility toward one another, for "God opposes the proud but gives grace to the humble." (1 Peter 5:5b)

And finally, fellow worshipers, keep going strong.

And let us not grow weary of doing good, for in due season we will reap, if we do not give up. (Galatians 6:9)

NOTES

JEFF POLEN MUSIC

USING MUSIC, SPEAKING, TEACHING, AND TRAINING, WE ARE POINTING BELIEVERS AND NON-BELIEVERS TO JESUS CHRIST.

THE JEFF POLEN MUSIC MINISTRY IS AN INVALUABLE RESOURCE FOR THE LOCAL CHURCH AND A STEADY INSTRUMENT BEING USED POWERFULLY IN THE HANDS OF GOD TO DRAW UNBELIEVERS TO THE CROSS OF CHRIST —WHERE THEY CAN FIND GRACE, HOPE, AND PURPOSE THROUGH THE MATCHLESS LOVE OF GOD.

AS A FAMILY, OUR DEEPEST DESIRE IS TO HONOR THE LORD WITH THE UNIQUE GIFTS AND TALENTS THAT HE HAS GIVEN US. AS A RESULT, WE SPECIALIZE IN FOUR MAIN AREAS OF MINISTRY, INCLUDING:
- CHRISTIAN BASED SINGING AND SPEAKING
- HIGH QUALITY EVENT SOUND AND LIGHTING
- TAYLOR'S PLAYGROUND RECORDING STUDIO
- MUSIC AND MINISTRY TRAINING AND RESOURCES

TO LEARN MORE, VISIT: WWW.JEFFPOLENMUSIC.COM

BROOKE GEHMAN

ILLUSTRATOR

BROOKE GEHMAN JOINED IN THE EPIC ENDEAVOR OF BRINGING
THIS BOOK TO LIFE BY CREATING A FUN, ARTISTIC REPRESENTATION
OF EACH CHAPTER. HE IS AN AUTHENTIC MAN OF GOD, A DEVOTED
FOLLOWER OF CHRIST, AND AN AMAZING HUSBAND AND FATHER.
HE IS A GIFTED WORSHIP LEADER, AN INCREDIBLE ARTIST, AND A
POTTER BY TRADE.

WWW.GEHMANPOTTERY.COM

WANT MORE?

FOR MORE GREAT TITLES, VISIT: WWW.JPVPRESS.COM